Cooking in the Midwest

A Collection of Favorite Recipes from the Heartland

Nancy Lantz

Images Unlimited Publishing

Maryville, Missouri

All inquiries should be addressed to:
Images Unlimited Publishing
P. O. Box 305
Maryville, MO 64468
660-582-4279
info@imagesunlimitedpublishing.com
http://www.imagesunlimitedpublishing.com

Front cover photo: Vasstamasfoto | Dreamstime.com
Back cover photo: Inkaphotoimage | Dreamstime.com
Cover Design: Teresa Carter
Interior cover design: Teresa Carter

ISBN 978-0-930643-30-0

First Edition

Printed in the United States of America

Table of Contents

SALADS, SOUPS, SIDES

Salads

FRUIT SALADS
Layered Salad
Peachy Fruit Salad
Pepsi Cola Salad
Pineapple Cheese Salad
Summertime Salad
Waldorf Salad

VEGETABLE SALADS
Apple Cabbage Slaw
Cauliflower Slaw
Copper Pennies
Corn and Pea Salad
Favorite Bean Salad
Favorite Coleslaw
Kidney Bean Salad for a Crowd
Lemon Caesar Salad
Spinach Salad Dressing

MAIN DISH SALADS
Macaroni Salad
Oriental Salad
Rotini Vegetable Salad
Tortellini Salad

Soups
Jan's Cheesy Soup
Hash Brown Potato Soup
Kathie's Stew
SlowCooker Potato Soup
SlowCooker Red Pepper Soup
Taco Soup
Vegetable Beef Soup
Vegetable Soup

Sides
Corn Casserole
Egg Noodles
Fried Corn
Fried Green Tomatoes
Rice with Mushrooms
Roasted Asparagus
Roasted Potatoes
Scalloped Corn
Skillet Cabbage
Zucchini Patties

Fruit Salads

Peachy Fruit Salad

1 (21 ounce) can peach pie
   filling
1 (20 ounce) can pineapple
   chunks, drained
1 (11 ounce) can mandarin
   oranges, drained
2 medium bananas, sliced
1 cup green grapes, halved
1 cup miniature marshmallows

Stir all ingredients together and
refrigerate.

Pineapple Cheese Salad

1 (16 ounce) can chunk
   pineapple in own juice
1 tablespoon butter
1 tablespoon sugar
1 heaping tablespoon
   cornstarch
1 cup grated Longhorn
   cheese
2 to 3 cups miniature
   marshmallows

Drain the pineapple and thicken juice
with the butter, sugar, and cornstarch in
the microwave or in pan on stove. Cool.
Place pineapple chunks, cheese, and
marshmallows in a bowl. Fold in thickened pineapple juice mixture and refrigerate.

Layered Salad

1 (3 ounce) package cream
  cheese, softened
½ cup mayonnaise or salad
  dressing
24 large marshmallows
1 (8 ounce) can crushed
  pineapple, drained
1 (8 ounce) carton whipped
  topping
1 (3 ounce) package lemon
  gelatin
1 (3 ounce) package raspberry
  gelatin
3 cups hot water

Mix cream cheese and mayonnaise and set aside. Add 1 cup of hot water to the 24 marshmallows; stir to melt. Let cool slightly and fold into cream cheese mixture. Add pineapple and whipped topping. Place in an 8 x 8-inch dish and refrigerate.

Dissolve lemon gelatin in 1 cup hot water; let cool and pour over chilled mixture. Refrigerate until set. Dissolve raspberry gelatin in 1 cup hot water; let cool and pour over lemon gelatin and refrigerate until set.

Pepsi Cola Salad

2 (20 ounce) cans crushed
  pineapple
2 (15 ounce) cans dark sweet
  cherries
2 (3 ounce) packages cherry
  gelatin
1 bottle Pepsi Cola (2 cups)

Measure the juice from the fruit and add enough water to total 2 cups. Bring to boil. Add gelatin and stir to dissolve. Add Pepsi (2 cups) and chill until slightly thickened. Add fruit and pour into 8 x 8-inch pan and refrigerate.

Waldorf Salad

4 tart red medium apples, diced
1 tablespoon lemon juice
1 cup diced celery
1 cup seeded dark grapes
1 cup miniature marshmallows
¼ cup mayonnaise or salad
  dressing
¼ cup heavy cream, whipped
¼ cup walnuts

Sprinkle diced apples with lemon juice. Combine with celery, grapes, marshmallows, and mayonnaise. Fold in whipped cream. Chill. Add walnuts when ready to serve.

Summertime Salad

6 peaches, peeled, pitted,
   and chopped
1 pound strawberries, washed,
   hulled, and sliced
½ pound seedless red grapes
½ pound seedless green grapes
¼ cup granulated sugar to taste
¼ cup pecans, toasted

Dressing
½ cup orange juice
Juice of one lime
1 teaspoon ground ginger

Combine prepared fruit in a large serving bowl. Sprinkle with sugar and toss gently. To toast pecans, arrange chopped nuts in a single layer in a shallow pan. Bake 8 to 10 minutes or until toasted and fragrant, stirring after 5 minutes. Watch closely.

Combine ingredients for dressing and pour over fruit. Toss to combine. Cover and refrigerate. When ready to serve, top fruit with toasted pecans.

▬ *Vegetable Salads* ▬

Favorite Bean Salad

¾ cup sugar
⅓ cup vegetable oil
⅔ cup white vinegar
½ teaspoon pepper
1 tablespoon celery seed
1 (16 ounce) can green beans,
   drained
1 (16 ounce) can wax (yellow)
   beans, drained
1 (16 ounce) can red kidney
   beans, drained and washed
½ cup green pepper, chopped
1 medium onion, sliced

Mix sugar, vegetable oil, vinegar, pepper, and celery seed in a large bowl. Add beans, green pepper, and onion; toss to coat. Cover and refrigerate overnight.

Kidney Bean Salad for a Crowd

1 gallon kidney beans, drained
12 eggs, boiled and chopped
1 jar pimento
1 tablespoon mustard
Miracle Whip or salad dressing
   to moisten
Colby or Longhorn cheese,
   chunked

Mix all together and refrigerate.

Cauliflower Slaw

4 cups cauliflower flowerets
¼ cup chopped green pepper
¼ cup chopped onion
⅔ cup sour cream
3 tablespoons mayonnaise
1 teaspoon dry mustard
1 teaspoon sugar
1 teaspoon dill weed
Few drops hot pepper sauce
Salt and pepper
2 medium chopped tomatoes

In a large bowl, combine cauliflower, green pepper, and onion and set aside. Stir together sour cream, mayonnaise, mustard, sugar, dill, and hot sauce and season with salt and pepper. Gently stir dressing into vegetable mixture. Cover and chill several hours. Just before serving carefully stir in the tomatoes.

Copper Pennies

2 pounds carrots,
   sliced into rings
1 large onion, sliced thin
1 green pepper, chopped
1 (10 ounce) can tomato soup
1 cup sugar
½ cup vinegar
⅓ cup salad oil
1 teaspoon Worcestershire
   sauce
1 teaspoon prepared mustard
Salt and pepper to taste

Cook carrots slightly, and then layer carrots, onions, and green pepper in a glass dish. Bring remaining ingredients to a boil; pour over vegetables. Let cool overnight. This will keep for up to two weeks in the refrigerator.

Corn and Pea Salad

5 cups frozen peas, cooked
   and drained
5 cups frozen corn, cooked and
   drained
1 cup celery, chopped
1 ½ cups crisp bacon,
   crumbled

Dressing
1 ½ cup Italian dressing,
   prepared
½ cup minced onion
¾ cup sour cream

Mix and refrigerate.

Apple Cabbage Slaw

6 cups cabbage, shredded
3 medium red apples, chopped
1 (5 ounce) can evaporated
   milk
¼ cup lemon juice
1 tablespoon sugar
2 teaspoons grated onion
1 teaspoon celery salt
½ teaspoon salt
Dash pepper, optional

Toss cabbage and apples. Combine rest of ingredients and pour over cabbage and apples. Cover and refrigerate.

Favorite Coleslaw

1 head cabbage, shredded
⅔ cup sugar
⅓ cup vinegar
¼ teaspoon celery seed
1 teaspoon salt
½ teaspoon garlic salt
¾ cup oil
Dash pepper

Boil sugar, vinegar, celery seed, and salts for approximately 1 minute or until sugar is dissolved. Add oil, stir, and pour over cabbage. Can also use shredded carrots in slaw.

Spinach Salad Dressing

½ cup sugar (use less if you
    want)
½ teaspoon dry mustard
½ cup water
⅛ cup vinegar
1 egg, beaten

In small saucepan, add sugar, dry mustard, water, and vinegar. Bring to boil. Cool to room temperature. Add mixture to the beaten egg and stir well. Place back on stove and bring to a boil, stirring constantly. Cool. Use on spinach/mandarin oranges/onion salad.

▬ *Main Dish Salads* ▬

Tortellini Salad

1 package frozen cheese
   ravioli
1 cup frozen peas
½ cup chopped ham
½ cup Colby Jack cheese
½ cup diced onions
1 bottle of Hidden Valley
   Ranch dressing

Cook the cheese ravioli as directed on package (reserve hot water). Pour hot water over frozen peas to thaw, then drain. Add the remaining ingredients, mix well and refrigerate until ready to serve.

Rotini Vegetable Salad

1 (8 ounce) package rotini
1 cup broccoli flowerets
1 cup cauliflower flowerets
½ cup red bell pepper, diced
1 cup American cheese, diced
1 cup cucumber, diced
1 cup French dressing
   or favorite dressing

Cook rotini in 6 cup rapidly boiling salt water for 4 minutes; cover and remove from heat. Let set for 7 to 9 minutes. Drain and rinse with cold water. Combine rest of ingredients and add dressing, cover, and refrigerate for several hours.

Oriental Salad

1 head cabbage, shredded
3 to 4 green onions, chopped
1 package pork-flavored
   ramen noodles, crushed
½ cup slivered almonds
¼ cup sunflower seeds
½ cup vegetable oil
1 tablespoon sugar
½ teaspoon black pepper
1 flavor packet from ramen
   noodles
1 jar with a lid

Mix together cabbage, chopped green onions and crushed ramen noodles. Cover and place in refrigerator. Meanwhile, toast almonds and sunflower seeds for 4 to 5 minutes in 350°F oven, then cool. Place oil, sugar, pepper, and flavor packet from ramen noodles in the jar. Shake to mix. When ready to serve, add toasted nuts to salad and toss with dressing.

Macaroni Salad

1 pound macaroni,
   cooked as directed
1 (14 ounce) can sweetened
   condensed milk
⅓ cup vinegar
1 green pepper, chopped
2 cups mayonnaise
   (not Miracle Whip)
½ cup sugar
1 cup Longhorn cheese, cubed

Mix together and refrigerate.

Soups

Jan's Cheesy Vegetable Soup

1 (16 ounce) package frozen
    vegetables or 6 potatoes
8 cups milk
8 ounces Velveeta cheese,
    cubed
4 tablespoons (¼ cup) butter
4 tablespoons cornstarch

Cook vegetables or potatoes until they are tender, drain, and add milk. Heat, but do not boil; add cheese to the milk mixture. Melt butter; mix in cornstarch and add to soup to thicken.

Hash Brown Potato Soup

3 cups milk
1 (10.75 ounce) can cream of
    potato soup
2 cups frozen southern-style
    hash browns
1 cup shredded sharp
    Cheddar cheese
2 slices bacon, crumbled
¼ cup green onions, thinly
    sliced
Salt and pepper to taste

Mix milk and soup in a large saucepan. Stir in hash browns. Bring to a boil on high heat, stirring occasionally. Reduce heat to medium low. Simmer 10 minutes, stirring frequently. Top with cheese, crumbled bacon and onions. Serves 6. Goes great with crusty whole grain rolls.

Slow Cooker Potato Soup

6 large russet potatoes, peeled and cut into ½ inch cubes
1 large onion, chopped
3 (14.5 ounce) cans chicken broth with roasted garlic
4 tablespoons (¼ cup) butter
2 ½ teaspoons salt
1 ¼ teaspoons freshly ground pepper
1 cup whipping cream or half and half
1 cup shredded sharp Cheddar cheese
3 teaspoons chopped fresh chives
1 container sour cream (optional)
4 slices bacon, cooked and crumbled

Combine potatoes, onion, chicken broth, butter, and salt and pepper in a 5-quart slow cooker. Cover and cook on high 4 hours or on low 8 hours, or until potatoes are tender. Mash mixture until potatoes are coarsely chopped and soup is slightly thickened. Stir in cream, cheese, and chives. To serve, top with sour cream and sprinkle with bacon and more Cheddar cheese.

Slow Cooker Red Pepper Soup

1 tablespoon olive oil
1 small onion, chopped
2 garlic cloves, finely chopped
1 teaspoon smoked paprika
4 medium-size red peppers, seeded and cut into 1 inch pieces (about 4 cups)
3 cups chicken broth
1 teaspoon sugar
½ teaspoon salt
¼ teaspoon white pepper
Basil for garnish

Heat oil in a large nonstick skillet over medium heat. Cook onion and garlic for 3 minutes or until softened. Stir in paprika and cook for 2 minutes. Add red pepper to skillet and cook, stirring occasionally, for 4 minutes. Scrape contents of skillet into slow-cooker and add chicken broth. Cover and cook on high for 3 hours or until red peppers are completely soft.

Puree soup in a blender, working with small batches at a time. Stir in seasonings. Cover and chill overnight. Can be served hot or cold. Garnish each serving with basil.

Taco Soup

1 pound ground beef or turkey
Chopped onion (optional)
2 (16 ounce) cans tomatoes
2 (16 ounce) cans kidney
   beans
1 (15 ounce) can tomato sauce
3 cups water
1 (1 ounce) envelope taco
   seasoning

Brown meat in heavy Dutch oven. Add onions, if using. Drain. Add all other ingredients and bring to a boil. Simmer for a few minutes to blend flavors.

Serve with green onions, sour cream and shredded cheese for each person to add. Serve with tortilla chips.

Kathie's Stew

2 pounds beef chuck roast,
   cut in 1 inch cubes
3 medium potatoes, quartered
3 medium carrots, ½ inch slices
1 (10 ounce) bag frozen green
   peas
1 cup onion, chopped
1 (10.75 ounce) can tomato
   soup
½ soup can water
¼ cup red wine
¼ cup flour
1 teaspoon salt
¼ teaspoon pepper
1 bay leaf

Heat oven to 275°F and mix all ingredients in a 3-quart casserole or Dutch oven. Cover and bake for 5 hours.

Mushroom and Barley Soup

8 cups water or beef or
　　chicken stock
1 cup pearl barley
1 cup coarsely chopped onion
1 cup coarsely chopped carrots
1 cup coarsely chopped
　　parsnips
½ ounce dried porcini
　　mushrooms
1 pound fresh mushrooms,
　　any kind
Salt and pepper to taste.

Add water or stock to large pot and bring to boil. Add barley, onions, carrots, and parsnips. Turn heat to low and partially cover. Keep at a low simmer.

Cover dried mushrooms with warm water and let soak about 10 minutes.

Wash and trim the fresh mushrooms and add to the simmering soup. Then add the dried mushrooms, along with their soaking liquid. Continue simmering the soup 30 to 45 minutes until barley and vegetables are tender. Season with salt and pepper. Garnish with parsley or chives.

Vegetable Beef Soup

3 pounds hamburger
1 large onion, peeled, and
　　chopped
1 package onion soup mix
1 (32 ounce) can chopped
　　tomatoes
1 (1 pound) package baby
　　carrots
¼ head cabbage, chopped
4 medium potatoes, peeled and
　　cubed
1 (10.5 ounce) can French
　　onion soup
2 (10.75 ounce) cans tomato
　　soup

In a Dutch oven, brown the hamburger and onion, then drain. Add remaining ingredients and bring to a boil. Reduce heat and simmer until vegetables are tender. Serve.

Vegetable Soup

1 (1 pound) package baby
   carrots
1 large onion, peeled and
   chopped
1 (16 ounce) can cut green
   beans
1 (16 ounce) can sweet
   kernel corn
4 medium potatoes, peeled
   and cubed
2 stalks celery, diced
1 (16 ounce) can diced
   tomatoes
½ (16 ounce) package frozen
   corn
½ (16 ounce) package frozen
   cauliflower
1 (10.75 ounce) can tomato
   soup
1 (11.5 ounce) can tomato juice
2 beef bouillon cubes
Salt and pepper to taste

Place all ingredients in a Dutch oven.
Add enough water to cover vegetables.
Bring to a boil and reduce heat. Cover
and simmer until vegetables are tender.

Sides

Roasted Asparagus

1 pound asparagus, trimmed
1 tablespoon olive oil
Salt and freshly ground black
  pepper
6 to 8 paper-thin slices ham,
  optional

Preheat the oven to 400°F. Trim stem ends off asparagus and place on a heavy baking sheet. Drizzle with olive oil, sprinkle with salt and pepper, and toss. Roast until the asparagus is tender, about 15 minutes. Serve hot or at room temperature.

For a variation, wrap each asparagus with a half slice cooked ham or Prosciutto. Arrange on platter.

Skillet Cabbage

1 tablespoon oil
3 cups cabbage, finely
  shredded
1 cup celery, chopped
1 small green pepper, chopped
½ teaspoon salt
Dash pepper

Heat oil in skillet over medium-low heat. Add remaining ingredients and stir until well mixed. Cover pan and cook 10 minutes or until vegetables are beginning to soften, stirring occasionally.

Scalloped Corn

1 (16 ounce) can cream style corn
1 (16 ounce) can whole kernel corn, undrained
1 (8.5) package corn muffin mix
½ cup (1 stick) butter, cut up
1 cup sour cream
1 teaspoon celery seed
Salt and pepper
Paprika

Mix together corn, corn muffin mix, butter, and sour cream. Add celery seed, and salt and pepper to taste. Sprinkle top with paprika and bake in large greased casserole at 350°F for 1 hour and 20 minutes.

Corn Casserole

1 (15 ounce) can creamed corn
1 (15 ounce) can whole kernel corn, undrained
1 cup Velveeta cheese
1 cup macaroni, uncooked
½ cup (1 stick) butter

Mix together all ingredients. Place in buttered casserole dish, cover, and bake at 350°F for 30 minutes. Uncover, stir, and bake uncovered for 30 more minutes, or until macaroni is softened.

Fried Corn

2 tablespoons butter
1 (16 ounce) package frozen corn or 2 cups fresh corn, about 6 ears
⅓ cup cream
2 tablespoons honey
Salt and pepper to taste

Melt butter in skillet and add rest of ingredients. Cook for 10 minutes or until heated through thoroughly.

Fried Green Tomatoes

8 (3 ½ pounds) medium green tomatoes
3 ½ teaspoons coarse salt
1 ¾ teaspoons freshly ground black pepper
3 cups flour
5 large eggs, beaten
½ cup milk
4 cups panko (Japanese breadcrumbs)
½ cup cornmeal
Oil for frying

Cut out stem ends and trim blossom ends of tomatoes. Slice tomatoes ¼ inch thick. Season slices with 2 teaspoons salt and 1 teaspoon pepper, set aside.

In a shallow bowl, whisk together flour, ½ teaspoon salt, and ½ teaspoon pepper; set aside.

In another shallow bowl, whisk together eggs and milk, set aside.

Place panko in a shallow pan along with cornmeal, remaining teaspoon salt, and ½ teaspoon pepper; stir to combine and set aside.

Set up a work station by lining up the tomatoes, flour mixture, egg mixture, and breadcrumb mixture. Working with one tomato slice at a time, coat tomatoes in each mixture, beginning with flour, then egg, then panko, and shaking off the excess each time.

Transfer coated tomatoes to a wire rack set over a parchment-lined baking sheet; repeat process with remaining slices.

Heat about ½ inch oil in a 10-skillet over medium heat until it reaches 350°F on a deep fry thermometer. Working in batches, carefully place tomatoes into the heated oil in a single layer. Fry until golden, turning once, 2 to 3 minutes per side. Drain on a paper towel-lined baking sheet.

Discard oil after frying half of the tomato slices and heat more oil in the skillet. Continue frying until all the tomato slices are golden and crisp. Serve immediately.

Roasted Potatoes

5 pounds red-skinned new
  potatoes
¾ cup extra-virgin olive oil
2 teaspoons coarse salt
Freshly ground black pepper
1 tablespoon finely minced
  garlic
½ cup coarsely chopped
  fresh mint leaves or ½ cup
  coarsely chopped parsley

Preheat oven to 350°F. Scrub the potatoes and prick each 3 or 4 times with a fork. Place in a single layer on a shallow roasting pan. Bake until tender, about 1 hour, depending on size of potatoes.

Cut the potatoes into halves or quarters and place them in a serving bowl. While still hot, toss them with the oil, salt, pepper, and garlic. Gently toss in the mint and/or parsley. Let rest for 30 minutes before serving.

Zucchini Patties

1 cup biscuit/baking mix
½ cup shredded Mozzarella
  or Cheddar cheese
⅛ teaspoon salt
2 eggs, beaten
2 cups zucchini, shredded
2 tablespoons onion, chopped
1 tablespoon butter

Combine baking mix, cheese, salt, eggs, zucchini, and onion in a mixing bowl. Blend well. Melt butter in a large skillet. Spoon heaping tablespoons of zucchini mixture into skillet. Fry for 3 to 5 minutes per side until golden brown. Drain on paper towel. Add more butter to skillet when needed.

Rice with Mushrooms

1 (10 ounce) can French
  onion soup
1 (10 ounce) can beef
  consommé
1 (4 ounce) can mushrooms,
  drained
½ cup (1 stick) butter
2 cups Minute Rice

Place all ingredients in a 2-quart microwave safe dish and microwave 10 minutes.

Egg Noodles

2 cups flour
Pinch salt
3 egg yolks
1 whole egg
¼ to ½ cup water
1 teaspoon vinegar

Mix the flour and salt in a bowl. Beat yolks and whole egg together and add ¼ cup water and 1 teaspoon vinegar. Add to flour and salt. Mix and knead until smooth. If mixture is too dry, add enough water to make dough bind together. Roll out on floured surface until ⅛ inch thick. Roll up jelly-roll style. Cut into ¼ inch slices. Unroll slices and cut noodles to desired length. May cook as desired or dry and place into a Ziplock bag and freeze until needed.

BREADS

Banana Bread
Banana Bread
Banana Nut Bread
Butterhorn Rolls
Cheddar & Roasted Garlic
  Biscuits
Cheddar Garlic Biscuits
Cinnamon Buns

Ground Cinnamon Bread
Ground Cinnamon Rolls
Easy in a Pinch Rolls
Honey Oat Casserole Bread
Hors d'oeuvres
Jiffy Yeast Bread
Oatmeal Rolls
Orange Knots
Poppy Seed Bread
Raisin-Pecan Ground Cinnamon
  Rolls
Rye Bread
Sticky Monkey Bread
Tea Ring
White Country Bread
Zucchini Bread
Zucchini Bread with Pudding Mix

Quick Breads

Hors d'oeuvres (Appetizer)

Toast bread and cut into quarters. Top with a slice of tomatoe and then a slice of round mozzarella cheese. Drizzle with olive oil. Salt and pepper to taste. Add dash of ground basil leaves.

Cheddar and Roasted Garlic Biscuits

5 cups biscuit/baking mix
1 cup shredded Cheddar cheese
1 (14 ½ ounce) can seasoned chicken broth with roasted garlic

Mix biscuit/baking mix, cheese, and broth to form soft dough. Drop by spoonful onto ungreased baking sheets and bake according to package directions. Makes 24 biscuits.

Tip: Freeze baked biscuits. To reheat, wrap in aluminum foil and heat at 375°F.

Cheddar Garlic Biscuits

2 cups biscuit/baking mix
⅔ cup milk
½ cup shredded Cheddar cheese
2 tablespoons melted butter
⅛ teaspoon garlic powder

Preheat oven to 450°F.

Mix first 3 ingredients to form soft dough. Drop by spoonful onto ungreased baking sheet.

Bake 8 to 10 minutes. Mix butter and garlic powder; brush over warm biscuits. Makes 9 biscuits.

Sticky Monkey Bread

4 cans (10 count) biscuits
1 cup sugar
2 teaspoons ground cinnamon

¾ cup (1 ½ sticks) butter
1 cup brown sugar
1 teaspoon ground cinnamon
1 cup chopped pecans

Lightly grease Bundt pan. Cut biscuits into quarters. Drop into bag with 1 cup sugar and 2 teaspoons ground cinnamon. Shake to coat, and layer biscuits into pan. Melt butter and 1 cup brown sugar, then add 1 teaspoon ground cinnamon and 1 cup chopped pecans. Pour over biscuits.

Bake at 350°F for 30 to 35 minutes. Cool for 10 minutes. Then invert on serving dish. Serve warm.

Cinnamon Swirled Bread

1 cup (2 sticks) butter, softened
2 cups sugar
2 eggs
4 cups all-purpose flour
2 teaspoons baking soda
2 cups buttermilk (or 2 cups
   milk plus 2 tablespoons
   lemon juice or vinegar)

Cinnamon/Sugar Mixture
⅔ cup sugar
2 teaspoons ground cinnamon

Preheat oven to 350°F.
Grease two 9 x 5 x 3-inch loaf pans.

Cream butter and sugar. Add eggs and beat. Gradually add flour and baking soda alternately with buttermilk or sour milk, beginning and ending with flour. Mix just until combined. Pour half the batter into two greased loaf pans. (Each pan will have ¼ of the total batter).

Mix together sugar and cinnamon and sprinkle ¾ of this mixture over the top of the batter in each pan. Pour remaining batter into each pan and sprinkle with remaining cinnamon mixture. Then swirl with knife through batter.

Bake at 350°F for 45 to 55 minutes. Cool at least 15 minutes before removing from pan.

Cinnamon Buns

2 ½ cups all-purpose flour
2 ½ teaspoons baking powder
½ teaspoon baking soda
½ teaspoon salt
¼ cup sugar
3 tablespoons shortening
1 cup sour milk (add 2
    tablespoons vinegar to
    milk to sour)

Cinnamon Mixture
¼ cup white sugar
¼ cup brown sugar
½ cup (1 stick) butter or
    margarine
2 teaspoons ground cinnamon
Small amount of honey

Mix dry ingredients. Cut in shortening. Add sour milk. Mix well. Knead and roll out as for cinnamon rolls.

Spread with Cinnamon Mixture. Roll and cut into buns. Place on well-greased baking sheet. Bake at 350°F for 12 to 15 minutes.

Basic Banana Nut Bread

¼ cup (½ stick) butter, melted
1 cup sugar
2 eggs, beaten
1 teaspoon vanilla
1 cup mashed banana
1 ½ cups all-purpose flour
1 teaspoon baking soda

Cream butter and sugar. Add beaten eggs and vanilla. Stir in banana. Sift dry ingredients. Fold into first mixture. Stir only until well blended. Spoon into well-greased loaf pan.

Bake at 375°F for 25 to 35 minutes.

Banana Bread

1 cup (2 sticks) butter
1 cup sugar
2 eggs (separated)
3 to 4 large bananas (mashed)
2 cups all-purpose flour
1 teaspoon baking soda
¼ teaspoon salt
1 cup chopped nuts

Cream butter, sugar, egg yolks, and bananas.

Sift together flour, baking soda, and salt.

Mix into butter/sugar/banana mixture.

Beat egg whites until peaks form. Gently fold beaten egg whites into batter. Spoon into well-greased loaf pan.

Bake at 350°F until done, about 50 to 60 minutes.

Banana Bread/Sweetened Condensed Milk

½ cup (1 stick) butter
1 cup sugar
1 egg beaten
½ teaspoon baking soda
3 tablespoons sweetened
  condensed milk
1 cup mashed bananas
2 cups sifted all-purpose flour
1 teaspoon baking powder
½ cup walnuts

Cream butter and sugar. Add beaten egg. Dissolve soda in milk and stir in bananas. Add to creamed mixture and mix in flour and baking powder which have been sifted together. Fold in nuts. Spoon into greased and floured loaf pans.

Bake 40 minutes at 350°F.

Poppy Seed Bread

3 cups all-purpose flour
2 ½ cups sugar
1 ½ teaspoons baking powder
1 ½ teaspoons salt
1 ½ cups oil
1 ½ cups milk
3 eggs
1 ½ tablespoons poppy seed
1 ½ teaspoons vanilla
1 ½ teaspoons butter, melted

Glaze
1 teaspoon butter, melted
1 teaspoon vanilla
¼ cup orange juice
¾ cup sugar

In large bowl measure and whisk in dry ingredients. Add oil, milk, and eggs. Beat until well blended. Sprinkle in poppy seeds. Add vanilla and melted butter. Mix just until blended.

Spoon into a well-greased or sprayed loaf pan. Bake at 350°F for 60 to 70 minutes. Pour glaze over hot bread and let soak in. Cool on wire rack.

Zucchini Bread

2 cups sugar
1 cup oil
3 eggs
2 cups grated zucchini
2 cups all-purpose flour
½ teaspoon baking soda
1 teaspoon salt
2 tablespoons ground
    cinnamon
½ cup chopped nuts, optional

Thoroughly mix the first 3 ingredients. Then add the remaining ingredients. Grease and flour 2 loaf pans. Fill ⅔ full.

Bake at 350°F for 1 hour. Add nuts if desired.

Zucchini Bread with Pudding Mix

3 eggs (beaten)
1 cup cooking oil
2 cups sugar
1 (3.4 ounce) package vanilla
   instant pudding
2 cups grated zucchini
2 teaspoons vanilla
3 cups all-purpose flour
½ teaspoon baking powder
1 teaspoon baking soda
1 teaspoon salt
1 teaspoon ground cinnamon
½ cup chopped nuts (optional)

Preheat oven at 325°F. Grease and flour 2 large loaf pans.

In large bowl, beat together eggs and oil. Stir in sugar, pudding, zucchini, and vanilla. Sift dry ingredients and add to zucchini mixture. Mix well by hand until all flour is moistened. Add nuts. Mixture will be thick.

Spoon into greased loaf pans. Bake at 325°F for 1 hour. Test with clean toothpick in center of loaf for doneness.

Yeast Breads

Orange Knots

1 package active dry yeast
¼ cup warm water
⅓ cup sugar
1 cup milk, scalded
½ cup (1 stick) butter, softened
1 teaspoon salt
2 eggs
¼ cup orange juice
2 tablespoon grated orange
   peel
5 ¼ to 5 ¾ cups all-purpose
   flour

Frosting
1 cup powdered sugar
2 tablespoons orange juice
1 teaspoon grated orange peel

Dissolve yeast in warm water in small bowl; add sugar. Scald milk and cool to lukewarm. Add butter and salt to warm milk. In large bowl, combine yeast mixture and warm milk mixture. Beat in eggs, orange juice, and orange peel. Slowly add 3 cups flour and beat until smooth. Add enough flour to form soft dough. Turn onto a floured board and knead until smooth and elastic. Place in a greased bowl, turning once to grease the top. Cover and let rise in a warm place until doubled in size.

When doubled in size, punch down lightly. Roll into 16 x 10-inch rectangle, about ½ inch thick. Cut into 10 inch x 3 ¼-inch stripes; roll lightly and tie into a knot. Place on greased baking sheet and tuck ends under. Let rise until double in size.

Bake at 400°F for 10 to 12 minutes. Cool, and then drizzle frosting over rolls.

Monica's Rye Bread

1 cup plus 2 tablespoons water
¾ cup rye flour
2 ¾ cups all-purpose flour
1 tablespoon gluten
1 ½ teaspoons active dry yeast
1 tablespoon brown sugar
1 teaspoon honey in ¼ cup
    molasses
1 teaspoon salt
2 tablespoons butter or
    margarine

Set the bread machine according to directions and set on 2. You can just let the machine do the mixing and let it rise and bake if you wish.

I usually let it rise in a greased bowl, then punch down lightly and put in a greased bread pan.

Let rise again and bake at 375°F for 20 minutes. Turn oven down to 325°F for another 15 to 20 minutes longer.

Monica's Tea Ring

½ cup milk, scalded
¼ cup sugar
1 teaspoon salt
¼ cup (½ stick) butter
    or margarine
½ cup warm water
2 packages active dry yeast
2 eggs, beaten
4 ½ cups all-purpose flour
    (or until sticky dough)

Butter, melted
Ground cinnamon
Sugar

Scald the milk. Stir in sugar, salt, and butter or margarine. Sprinkle yeast over warm water in large bowl. Add milk mixture, eggs, and half the flour. Beat until smooth. Stir in the remaining flour and knead well. Put in a greased bowl and let rise until double in bulk.

Roll out to a rectangle and spread with melted butter or margarine, ground cinnamon, and sugar. Roll up like jelly roll and arrange in a circle on a greased tea ring pan or baking sheet. Cut ⅔ into the ring with scissors at 1-inch intervals. Turn each piece over on its side and let rise until double in size. Bake at 325°F for 20 to 25 minutes. Frost while still warm.

Honey Oat Casserole Bread

1 package active dry yeast
¼ cup warm water
¼ cup (½ stick) butter,
  softened
¼ cup honey
1 cup boiling water
2 eggs
1 cup oatmeal, quick
1 teaspoon salt
3 ½ cups all-purpose flour

In a large mixer bowl dissolve yeast in warm water. In another bowl combine butter, honey, and boiling water. Stir until butter is melted. Cool. To the yeast mixture, add eggs, oats, salt, cooled butter mixture, and 2 cups flour. Mix. Stir in enough remaining flour to form soft dough. Mixture will be slightly sticky. Cover and let rise until double in size. Punch dough down. Transfer to a greased 1 ½ quart round baking dish. Cover and let rise in a warm place until double in size.

Bake at 375°F for 35 to 40 minutes until golden brown. Cool 10 minutes before removing from baking dish to a wire rack to cool. Cut in wedges.

Jiffy Yeast Bread

1 ¼ cups warm water
1 package active dry yeast
1 (9 ounce) Jiffy cake mix
  (white)
2 ½ to 3 cups all-purpose flour

Combine all ingredients. Grease bowl. Turn dough to coat. Let rise once and then knead some. Make into rolls or bread and let rise again in well-greased pans.

Bake at 350°F for 12 to 15 minutes for rolls or until done.

Cinnamon Yeast Rolls

½ cup shortening
¼ cup sugar
1 egg
1 teaspoon salt
1 package active dry yeast
½ cup lukewarm water
1 cup water
4 cups all-purpose flour
Butter or margarine
Brown sugar
Ground cinnamon

Cream shortening and sugar, add egg and salt. Set aside.

In large mixing bowl, mix yeast and lukewarm water thoroughly, then add 1 cup water. Mix in yeast and water and creamed mixture with a spoon. Slowly add flour, knead slightly. Grease bowl and let rise.

Punch down and let rise again. Then roll out dough 1 inch thick. Spread with butter or margarine, brown sugar, and ground cinnamon. Roll up and cut into 1-inch rolls. Place in well-greased pans with a 1-inch space between each and let rise. Then bake at 375°F for 15 to 20 minutes.

Easy in-a-Pinch Rolls

2 ¼ cups all-purpose flour
2 tablespoons sugar
1 teaspoon salt
1 package active dry yeast
1 cup warm water
1 egg, beaten
2 tablespoons melted butter

In a large bowl, mix together flour, sugar, salt, and yeast. Add warm water, beaten egg, and melted butter. Gently combine just until moistened. Scoop dough out onto a floured board. Gently knead to pull the dough together. Do not over-knead the dough.

Spoon into greased muffin tins or alternately, use a cookie cutter and place rolls on greased baking sheet. Gently spread with softened butter or pour melted butter on top of the rolls. Let rise until double in size. Bake at 400°F for 15 minutes. Makes 12 rolls.

Raisin-Pecan Cinnamon Rolls

4 ½ to 5 cups all-purpose flour
1 package active dry yeast
1 cup milk
⅓ cup butter or margarine
⅓ cup sugar
½ teaspoon salt
3 eggs

Filling

¾ cup brown sugar
¼ cup all-purpose flour
1 tablespoon ground cinnamon
½ cup (1 stick) butter or
    margarine
½ cup light raisins
½ cup chopped pecans
1 tablespoon half-and-half or
    light cream

Powdered Sugar Glaze

1 ¼ cups sifted powdered
    sugar
1 teaspoon corn syrup
½ teaspoon vanilla
1 to 2 tablespoons half-and-half
    or light cream

In a large mixer bowl combine 2 ¼ cups of the flour and the yeast. In small saucepan heat the milk, the ⅓ cup butter or margarine, ⅓ cup sugar, and salt just until warm (120 degrees to 130 degrees) and butter or margarine is almost melted, stirring constantly. Add to flour mixture. Add eggs. Beat with an electric mixer on low speed for 30 seconds, scraping sides of bowl constantly. Beat on high speed for 3 minutes.

Using wooden spoon, stir in as much of the remaining 2 ¼ to 2 ¾ cups of flour as you can. Turn dough out onto a lightly floured surface. Knead in enough of the remaining flour to make moderately soft dough that is smooth and elastic (3 to 5 minutes total). Shape into a ball. Place in a greased bowl, turning once. Cover, and let rise in a warm place until double in size.

For filling, combine brown sugar, the ¼ cup flour, and ground cinnamon. Cut in remaining butter or margarine until crumbly. Set aside.

Instructions continued on next page.

After dough has doubled in size, punch down. Turn onto a lightly floured surface. Cover and let rest for 10 minutes. Then roll the dough into a 12-inch square. Sprinkle filling over dough square, top with raisins and pecans. Roll up jelly-roll style, pinch edges to seal. Slice roll into eight 1 ½ inch pieces, cut side up, in a greased 12-inch deep dish pizza pan or a 13 x 9-inch baking pan. Cover dough loosely with clear plastic wrap, leaving room for rolls to rise. Refrigerate for 2 to 24 hours.

Uncover and let stand at room temperature for 30 minutes. Break any surface bubbles with a greased toothpick. Brush dough with half-and-half or light cream. Bake in a 350°F oven for 20 minutes or until light brown. If necessary to prevent over browning, cover rolls loosely with foil the last 5 to 10 minutes of baking.

Remove rolls from oven. Brush again with half-and half or light cream. Cool for 1 minute. Carefully invert ground cinnamon rolls onto a wire rack. Cool slightly. Invert again onto a serving platter. Drizzle with powdered sugar glaze.

In a bowl, stir together ingredients. Use just enough half-and-half or light cream to make a drizzling consistency. Serve warm. Makes 8 rolls.

Butterhorn Rolls

1 package active dry yeast
1 ¼ cups warm water
½ cup sugar
½ cup melted shortening
1 ½ teaspoons salt
3 eggs, beaten
4 ½ to 5 cups all-purpose flour
Butter, melted

Dissolve yeast in warm water. Add sugar, melted shortening, salt and beaten eggs. Mix. Gradually stir in flour. Knead for 5 minutes. Cover and let rise until double in size.

Punch down and divide dough into thirds. Roll each section into a circle ¼ inch thick.

Spread with melted butter. Cut each circle into 8 pie shaped pieces. Roll into crescent shaped rolls and place on greased baking sheet. Let rise for 45 minutes.

Bake at 350°F for 10 minutes. Brush with butter.

Oatmeal Rolls

1 cup oatmeal (regular)
2 cups boiling water
3 tablespoons butter
1 tablespoon sugar
2 packages yeast, dissolved in
    ⅓ cup warm water
⅔ cup brown sugar
1 ½ teaspoons salt
5 cups all-purpose flour

Combine oatmeal, boiling water, butter, and sugar. Stir and let set for 10 minutes.

In large bowl, dissolve yeast in warm water. Add oatmeal mixture, brown sugar, salt, and half the flour. Beat until smooth. Add enough remaining flour to form a soft dough. Turn out on floured surface and knead for 6 to 8 minutes. Let rise until double, approximately 45 minutes to 1 hour.

Punch down and form into rolls or loaves and place in greased pans. Let rise again until double. Bake at 350°F for 20 to 25 minutes.

White Country Bread

2 packages active dry yeast
2 cups warm water
½ cup sugar
1 tablespoon salt
2 eggs, beaten
¼ cup vegetable oil
7 cups all-purpose flour,
   divided

In a large mixing bowl, dissolve yeast in warm water. Add sugar, salt, eggs, oil, and 3 ½ cups of flour. Beat until smooth. Sift in enough remaining flour to form soft dough and turn onto a floured surface. Knead until it is smooth and elastic, about 7 minutes. Place in a greased bowl and turn once to grease the top.

Cover and let rise in a warm place until doubled in size, about an hour.

Punch dough down and divide in half, then shape into two loaves or approximately 16 dinner rolls. Place in greased pans. Cover and let rise until doubled in size.

Bake at 375°F for 25 to 30 minutes or until golden brown. Brush with melted butter, and remove from pans, cool on wire racks.

MAIN DISHES

BBQ Beef Short Ribs
BBQ Meatballs
BBQ Short Ribs
Beef Brisket
Beef/Broccoli Stir Fry
Breakfast on the Grill
Cassie's Egg Rolls
Chicken with Eggplant and
    Veggies
Chicken Enchilada
Chicken Fajitas
Chicken Rice Bake
Chili Fritos
Chinese Chicken
Crab Casserole
Crab-Stuffed Trout
Creole Baked Fish
Crispy Oven-Fried Tortilla
    Chip-Crusted Chicken
Country Style Beef Stew
Favorite Meatloaf
Flank Steak

French Toast Casserole
German Spareribs
Grilled Pork Loin Roast
Homemade Chili for a Group
Kielbasa & Pepper Casserole
Leftover Rotisserie Chicken and
    Extra Shrimp
Lemon-Dill Tilapia
Mac 'n Cheese with Bacon
Maid Rite-Like Hamburgers for a
    Large Group
Meatballs
Mexican Stuff Shells
Mushroom Chicken Strips
Mustard & Soy Glazed Salmon
Overnight French Toast Casserole
Pork Chop Supreme
Pork Tortillas
Portobello Mushroom Lasagna
Pulled Pork Sandwiches
Sausage Balls
Seasoned Meatloaf
Simple Salisbury Steak
Spiced-Up Flank Steak
Stuffed Green Peppers
Swiss Steak
Texas Chicken Picante
Two-Cheese Macaroni Casserole
Valentino's Pizza Taste-Alike
Vegetable Combo Casserole
Vegetable Soup Meatloaf
Veggie Pizza

BEEF

Chili Fritos
Homemade Chili for a Group
Meatballs
BBQ Meatballs
Maid Rite-Like Hamburgers
   for a Large Group
Favorite Meatloaf
Seasoned Meatloaf
Vegetable Soup Meatloaf
Simple Salisbury Steak
Mexican Stuffed Shells
Cassie's Egg Rolls
Stuffed Green Peppers
Flank Steak
Spiced-Up Flank Steak
Barbecued Beef Short Ribs
German Spareribs
Beef Brisket
Swiss Steak
Country-Style Beef Stew
Beef/Broccoli Stir Fry

PORK

Sausage Balls
Kielbasa and Pepper Casserole
Pork Tortillas
Pulled Pork Sandwiches
Grilled Pork Loin Roast
Pork Chop Supreme
Mac 'n Cheese with Bacon

CHICKEN

Chicken Fajitas
Mushroom Chicken Strips
Chicken Enchilada
Chicken Rice Bake
Chicken with Eggplant and Veggies
Leftover Rotisserie Chicken and
   Extra Shrimp
Texas Chicken Picante
Chinese Chicken
Crispy Oven-Fried Tortilla
   Chip-Crusted Chicken

FISH

Creole Baked Fish
Mustard and Soy Glazed Salmon
Lemon-Dill Tilapia
Crab-Stuffed Trout
Crab Casserole

VEGETARIAN

Vegetable Combo Casserole
Veggie Pizza
Valentino's Pizza Taste-Alike
Portobello Mushroom Lasagna
Two-Cheese Macaroni Casserole

BREAKFAST

Breakfast on the Grill
French Toast Casserole

Beef

Chili Fritos

2 pounds hamburger
1 onion, chopped
2 (15 ounce) cans chili beans
2 tablespoons chili powder
1 (10 ounce) can Rotel diced
    tomatoes and green chilies
1 clove garlic
1 tablespoon sugar
1 teaspoon oregano
1 teaspoon ground cumin
Individual bags of Fritos
Shredded sharp Cheddar
    cheese

Brown hamburger with onion; drain. Add the rest of the ingredients, bring to a boil. Decrease the heat and simmer for 30 minutes. Stir occasionally.

To serve, slice open Frito bags lengthwise. Add chili and shredded cheese. Add fork and serve immediately.

Homemade Chili for a Group

10 pounds ground beef
4 large onions, chopped,
    browned with ground beef
    and drained well
2 gallons red beans, drained
1 ¾ cups chili seasoning
3 teaspoons salt
½ cup sugar
5 (46 ounce) cans tomato juice
6 cups hot water

Brown ground beef and onions; drain. Mix in rest of ingredients and heat thoroughly.

To serve, slice open Frito bags lengthwise. Add chili and shredded cheese. Add plastic fork and serve immediately.

Meatballs

1 ½ - 2 pounds hamburger
¾ cup evaporated milk
1 tablespoon onion flakes
½ teaspoon salt
¼ teaspoon pepper
1 ½ cups oatmeal, quick

Sauce
3 tablespoons Worcestershire
    sauce
3 tablespoons vinegar
1 cup ketchup

Mix ingredients together and shape into about 40 balls.

Brown them in a skillet and then drain. Make sauce, pour over meatballs, and let simmer at least 20 minutes. The longer the meatballs stay in the sauce the better they taste.

BBQ Meatballs

1 ½ pounds hamburger
6 ounces evaporated milk
1 cup oatmeal, quick
½ cup chopped onion
¼ teaspoon garlic powder
1 teaspoon salt
¼ teaspoon pepper

Sauce
1 cup ketchup
¾ cup brown sugar
1 tablespoon liquid smoke or
    any BBQ sauce
¼ teaspoon garlic powder
¼ cup chopped onion

Mix together and shape into balls. Place in a shallow pan in a single layer.

Cover with foil and bake at 350°F for 30 minutes. Uncover, drain grease and pour sauce on meatballs. Bake for another 30 minutes uncovered.

Maid Rite-Like Hamburgers for a Large Group

10 pounds hamburger
1 (10.75 ounce) can tomato
  soup
1 (6 ounce) can tomato paste
3 teaspoons chili powder
3 teaspoons dry mustard
6 teaspoons salt
1 large onion, finely chopped

In large container, add ingredients to hamburger and simmer. Serve loose hamburger meat on buns. Serves 80 - 100.

Favorite Meatloaf

2 eggs
¼ cup milk
1 tablespoon Worcestershire
  sauce
1 teaspoon seasoned salt
1 teaspoon onion powder
1 cup oatmeal, quick
1 carrot, shredded
2 tablespoons parsley,
  chopped
1 ½ pounds ground beef
1 pound ground pork
½ cup ketchup

Beat eggs, add milk and Worcestershire sauce, salt, and onion powder, and mix well. Stir in oatmeal, carrots, and parsley. Add beef and pork to the egg mixture and mix well. Press into 9 x 5-inch loaf pan. Top with ketchup. Bake at 350°F degrees for 1 ½ hours or until no pink remains in the middle.

Cassie's Egg Rolls

2 pounds hamburger
½ cup celery, chopped
½ cup carrots, diced
1 green pepper, diced
2 garlic cloves
1 medium onion
8 egg roll wraps
Oil for deep-fat frying

Brown and drain hamburger. Mix in vegetables with meat and cook for 10 minutes, then spoon into egg rolls and wrap. Deep-fat fry until brown, turning occasionally until golden brown. Remove from oil and drain on paper towels.

Seasoned Meatloaf

2 pounds ground beef
1 cup bread crumbs
  (seasoned)
1 (1 ounce) package onion
  soup mix
5 tablespoons ketchup
2 tablespoons prepared
  mustard
2 eggs
⅓ to ½ teaspoon salt
½ teaspoon pepper

Sauce
½ cup sugar
4 tablespoons brown sugar
2 to 3 tablespoons vinegar
5 tablespoons ketchup

Combine all ingredients and put into baking dish. Bake at 350°F for 1 ½ hours and then drain. Spoon sauce over the cooked meatloaf and bake 10 more minutes.

Vegetable Soup Meatloaf

2 slices white bread, torn
1 (10.75 ounce) can
  condensed vegetarian
  vegetable soup, undiluted
1 small onion, chopped
1 egg, beaten
½ teaspoon salt
⅛ teaspoon pepper
1 ½ pounds lean ground beef
1 (10.75 ounce) can tomato
  soup

In a large bowl, soak bread in soup for 5 minutes. Stir in the onion, egg, salt, and pepper. Crumble beef over mixture and mix well. Shape into an 8 x 4-inch loaf-pan. Line an 11 x 7-inch baking dish with foil and grease the foil*. Place meatloaf in pan; top with tomato sauce. Bake, uncovered at 350°F for 50 to 60 minutes or until a meat thermometer reads 160°F. Let stand for 10 minutes before slicing.

*Shaping first in the smaller loaf-pan and then placing in larger pan will allow the grease to flow out from all sides. It will be easier to transfer to a serving platter.

Simple Salisbury Steak

1 (10.75 ounce) can cream of
  mushroom soup
1 pound ground beef
⅓ cup bread crumbs
1 egg, beaten
¼ cup chopped onion
1 ½ cups mushrooms

In a bowl, mix ¼ cup soup, ground beef, bread crumbs, egg, and onion. Shape into patties. In skillet over medium high heat, cook patties, a few at a time, until browned on both sides. Spoon off any extra fat. Stir in remaining soup and mushrooms, and return patties to skillet. Reduce heat to low heat and cover; simmer for 20 minutes or until done.

Mexican Stuffed Shells

1 pound ground beef, cooked
  and drained
1 (16 ounce) jar mild picante
  sauce
½ cup water
1 (8 ounce) can tomato sauce
1 (4 ounce) can chopped green
  chilies, drained
1 cup (4 ounce) shredded
  Monterey Jack cheese
1 (10 ounce) can French fried
  onions
12 (jumbo) stuffing shells

Brown beef. Combine picante sauce, water, and tomato sauce in a separate bowl and stir. Measure out ½ cup of the sauce and pour over ground beef. Then add green chilies, cheeses and half of the fried onions. Mix. Take half of the remaining sauce and pour in 8 x 12-inch baking dish.

Stuff shells with ground beef mixture. Arrange shells in baking dish; pour remaining sauce over shells. Bake covered at 350°F for 30 minutes. Top with remaining cheese and onions. Bake uncovered for 5 minutes longer.

Stuffed Green Peppers

4 green peppers
¾ pound ground beef
⅓ cup cooked rice
1 teaspoon salt
Dash of pepper
1 egg
1 onion, chopped
1 (10.75 ounce) can tomato
    soup

Slice off top and remove seeds from peppers. Place peppers in boiling water for 3 minutes. Combine ground beef, rice, salt, pepper, egg, onion, and ½ cup of tomato soup. Stuff peppers and replace top of green pepper and anchor with a toothpick. Place peppers in 2-quart baking dish and spoon the remaining tomato soup over the peppers. Bake uncovered at 350°F for 45-55 minutes.

Flank Steak

2 flank steaks
    (about 1 ½ pounds each)

Marinade
⅔ cup dry red wine
⅔ cup soy sauce
6 large cloves of garlic, peeled
    and minced
⅓ cup chopped flat-leaf parsley
Black pepper to taste, coarsely
    ground

Combine the marinade ingredients in a non-reactive bowl. Add the flank steaks and coat well with the marinade. Marinate the steaks, covered, in the refrigerator for 30 minutes or overnight, turning once.

Remove from the marinade and pat dry. Broil or grill the steaks over high heat, 3 inches from the heat source, for 4 minutes per side for medium-rare meat. Remove to a cutting board and let rest for 10 minutes. To serve, slice thinly on the diagonal and arrange on a board or platter.

Spiced-Up Flank Steak

1 flank steak (1 ½ pounds)

Marinade
⅔ cup brown sugar
⅔ cup reduced-sodium soy
    sauce
⅔ cup V-8 juice
2 tablespoons olive oil
2 tablespoons chili powder
4 cloves garlic, chopped
¼ teaspoon ground cumin

In a large re-sealable plastic bag, combine the brown sugar, soy sauce, V-8 juice, olive oil, chili powder, garlic, and cumin. Pour off half and save in a jar for later. Add the steak to the plastic bag and marinate in the refrigerator at least 8 hours or overnight.

Remove steak from bag and discard marinade. Heat a grill to medium-high. Grill steak for 5 to 6 minutes per side, until internal temperature reads 150°F on an instant-read thermometer. Remove steak from grill and cover with foil. Let stand 5 minutes before thinly slicing against the grain. Heat saved marinade and serve over steak.

Barbecued Beef Short Ribs

3 pounds beef short ribs
2 tablespoons bacon drippings
2 tablespoons onion, sliced
1 tablespoon green pepper,
    chopped
1 cup ketchup
1 teaspoon salt
1 teaspoon celery seed
2 tablespoons brown sugar
2 tablespoons lemon juice
2 teaspoons dry mustard
1 cup water

Brown the short ribs in drippings and pour off excess fat. Place ribs in a 9 x 13-inch baking dish. Mix remaining ingredients together and pour over ribs. Cover and bake at 325°F until ribs are tender.

Slow Cooker German Spareribs

2 ½ pounds spareribs
   (beef or pork)
1 tablespoon oil
1 teaspoon salt
Dash of pepper
1 (32 ounce) bag sauerkraut
1 tablespoon brown sugar
4 medium potatoes, peeled
   and quartered
⅔ cup water

Brown spareribs in oil. Add salt and pepper. Place sauerkraut in bottom of slow cooker. Sprinkle with brown sugar. Place ribs and potatoes over sauerkraut, add water, cover, and set control on low. Cook until ribs are tender.

Beef Brisket

3 to 4 pounds beef brisket
½ teaspoon each ground
   allspice, chili powder,
   garlic powder, onion powder,
   paprika, season salt, and
   sugar
¼ teaspoon pepper
½ cup cola
⅓ cup Worcestershire sauce
½ cup cider vinegar
½ cup (1 stick) butter
⅓ cup soy sauce
¾ cup barbeque sauce

Combine dry seasonings, cover, and set aside. Place meat in shallow dish or large resealable plastic bag. Mix cola and Worcestershire sauce; pour over meat, and cover and/or seal container. Refrigerate overnight and then drain meat. Discard marinade. Place meat in large shallow roasting pan and rub saved seasonings over meat.

Combine vinegar, butter, and soy sauce and pour over meat. Cover and bake at 325°F for 2 hours, basting occasionally. Drain meat and pour barbeque sauce over meat, cover, and bake until tender.

Swiss Steak

3 - 4 round steaks, tenderized
2 tablespoons olive oil
1 (10.75 ounce) can cream of
    mushroom soup
Onion and celery, chopped
1 (15 ounce) can tomatoes

In pan, add oil and brown meat. Meanwhile, heat together soup and chopped onion and celery. Spoon mixture over steak and top with tomatoes. Bake at 350°F until done (1 ½ - 2 hours).

Country-Style Beef Stew

1 ½ pounds stew beef
    (cut into cubes)
¼ cup flour
2 tablespoons oil
Salt and pepper to taste
2 (14 ½ ounce) cans stewed
    tomatoes
1 (13 ¾ ounce) can beef broth
4 medium carrots, pared,
    cut in 1-inch chunks
2 medium potatoes, pared,
    cut in 1-inch chunks
¾ teaspoon thyme
2 tablespoons Dijon mustard
Parsley, chopped

Combine meat and flour in plastic bag, toss to coat evenly. In 6-quart pot, brown meat in oil. Salt and pepper to taste. Add remaining ingredients, except mustard. Bring to boil, reduce heat. Cover and simmer 1 hour or until beef is tender. Blend in mustard. Garnish with chopped parsley and serve with crusty French bread.

Beef/Broccoli Stir Fry

¾ pounds lean beef
1 pound fresh broccoli
2 garlic cloves
¼ teaspoon salt, or to taste
⅛ teaspoon pepper, or to taste
½ teaspoon sugar, or to taste
2 tablespoons oil

Marinade

1 tablespoon rice vinegar
1 teaspoon sugar
1 teaspoon soy sauce
1 tablespoon water
1 tablespoon cornstarch

Sauce

2 tablespoons oyster sauce
1 tablespoon light soy sauce
1 tablespoon dark soy sauce
1 tablespoon water
1 teaspoon cornstarch mixed
   with 1 tablespoon water

Cut the beef across the grain into thin slices. Mix together the marinade ingredients in a bowl and add the meat. Marinate the beef for 30 minutes.

While the beef is marinating, prepare the sauce and vegetables. For the sauce, mix together the oyster sauce, soy sauces, and water in a small bowl. In a small cup, mix the 1 teaspoon cornstarch and 1 tablespoon water and add to sauce. Set aside. Wash broccoli and cut the stalk diagonally into slices. Cut the flowerets into bite-size pieces. Crush the garlic and set aside.

Heat the wok and add 1 to 2 tablespoons oil. When the oil is medium-hot (between 300 and 325°F) add beef in a single layer, about a cup at a time, laying the meat out flat to cook and allowing it to cook undisturbed for 30 to 60 seconds.

Then stir to separate the pieces. Stir fry only until beef changes color and is nearly cooked (the entire process takes 1 to 2 minutes). Add the crushed garlic and stir fry another minute, turning down the heat to make sure it doesn't burn. Remove the meat from the wok. (Cook meat in batches, if necessary.)

Wipe out wok with paper towels. Add broccoli; sprinkle with salt and pepper and sugar, if desired. Add about ¼ cup water and cover. Cook for 4 to 5 minutes or until it turns a bright green and is tender but still crisp. Add the meat back when the vegetables are almost cooked. Add the sauce and cornstarch mixture and stir quickly to thicken. Mix everything together and serve hot over steamed rice.

Pork

Sausage Balls

2 cups biscuit/baking mix
1 pound sausage
1 cup shredded Cheddar
  cheese

Mix all together; roll into balls size of a walnut. Bake at 350° F for 15 minutes or until brown. Can be frozen and then reheated.

Kielbasa and Pepper Casserole

½ pound smoked kielbasa or
  Polish sausage, cut into
  ½ inch slices
4 small red potatoes, halved
1 medium onion, halved and
  sliced
1 medium sweet red pepper,
  cut into 1-inch pieces
2 tablespoons olive oil
⅛ teaspoon salt
⅛ teaspoon pepper
¼ cup heavy whipping cream
Fresh parsley, minced

In a small bowl, combine the sausage, potatoes, onion, and red pepper. Drizzle with oil; sprinkle with salt and pepper. Toss to coat. Transfer to a greased 1 quart baking dish. Cover and bake at 375°F for 45 minutes. Stir in cream; cover and bake 10 to 15 minutes longer or until vegetables are tender and the cream has thickened. Sprinkle with parsley.

Pork Tortillas

1 pork tenderloin
  (about 12 ounces)
  trimmed of excess fat
2 teaspoons oil
1 tablespoon each minced
  fresh garlic and ginger
4 ounces shiitake mushrooms
  (discard stems) or white
  mushrooms, sliced
4 cups coleslaw mix
½ (14 ounce) can baby corn,
  ears cut in half lengthwise
⅓ cup seasoned rice-wine
  vinegar
¼ cup Chinese barbecue
  sauce
8 (7 to 8 inch) flour tortillas

Preheat oven to 425°F.

Cut pork crosswise into thin slices, then cut each slice in half. Place tortillas in a single layer on 2 large baking sheets.

Meanwhile, heat 1 teaspoon oil in a large nonstick skillet over medium-high heat and add half of the pork, garlic, and ginger. Stir-fry 1 to 2 minutes, or until pork is cooked through. Transfer to a bowl and repeat with remaining oil pork, garlic, and ginger.

Bake tortillas 4 to 5 minutes until somewhat brown. Meanwhile, add mushrooms to any drippings in skillet and stir-fry 2 minutes, or until lightly browned or tender. Add coleslaw mix, corn, and vinegar, then stir-fry for 1 to 2 minutes until cabbage wilts. Stir pork mixture and remove skillet from heat.

Remove tortillas to a wire rack (they will get crisp). Spread with Chinese barbecue sauce and top with pork mixture. Serve immediately.

Pork Chop Provencal

4 boneless pork chops,
   ½ inch thick
1 tablespoon olive oil
⅛ teaspoon salt
¼ teaspoon black pepper
½ cup dry white wine
2 cups chicken broth
1 (15 ounce) can tomatoes,
   broken or 2 large peeled
   ripe tomatoes
1 or 2 Spanish onions,
   chopped coarse
2 cloves garlic, minced
1 tablespoon grainy Dijon
   mustard
½ cup chopped fresh parsley

Heat oil in a large nonstick skillet over medium-high heat. Season pork chops with salt and pepper. Add to skillet and sear for 3 to 4 minutes, or until lightly browned. Remove to plate. Reduce heat to medium and add wine and broth, stirring up brown bits in pan. Cook few minutes. Stir in tomatoes, onions, garlic, and mustard. Cook 3 minutes, stirring occasionally.

Return meat to skillet. Stir. Cover skillet securely and cook over very low heat about 2 hours, or until meat is almost but not quite falling off the bone. Add more broth or water if necessary. Stir in parsley. To serve, spoon sauce over chops.

Slow Cooker Pulled Pork Sandwiches

1 boneless pork butt or
    shoulder (about 2 ½ pounds)
2 ½ tablespoons dark brown
    sugar
1 tablespoon paprika
1 teaspoon chili powder
1 teaspoon ground cumin
1 teaspoon black pepper
1 cup chicken broth
2 tablespoons cider vinegar
2 tablespoons ketchup
6 hamburger buns

In a small bowl, stir together 1 table-spoon of the brown sugar, 1 teaspoon paprika, chili powder, cumin, and pepper and set aside. Place pork on work surface and sprinkle on all sides with spice rub; rub well into meat. Wrap in plastic wrap and refrigerate for 1 hour or overnight.

Unwrap pork and place in slow cooker with chicken broth. Cover and cook on high for 6 hours or low for 8 hours. Remove pork from slow cooker and cut into large chunks. Let stand for 20 minutes or until cool enough to handle. While pork is cooling, pour cooking liquid into a fat separator cup. Pour the de-fatted liquid into small saucepan. Heat over medium-high heat. Whisk in vinegar, ketchup, and remaining 1 ½ table-spoons brown sugar. Cook until sugar has dissolved, about 2 minutes, and set aside. Using forks or your hands, pull meat into shreds, discarding excess fat, and place in bowl. Stir in sauce and put ½ cup meat on each bun.

Grilled Pork Loin Roast

2 ½ pounds pork loin
Soy marinade
1 (12 ounce) can soda pop

Pierce pork loin roast several times with a knife. Place pork loin in a large zip-top plastic freezer bag; pour soda pop and soy marinade over meat and turn to coat. Cover or seal, and chill 4 to 6 hours, turning occasionally.

Light one side of grill, heating to 350° to 400°F; leave other side unlit. Remove roast from marinade, discarding marinade. Pat roast dry, and sprinkle with 1 teaspoon salt and ½ teaspoon pepper. Tie with kitchen string securing at 2-inch intervals. Place roast over lit side of grill, and grill, covered with grill lid, 5 minutes on each side or until browned.

Transfer roast to other side, and grill, covered with grill lid, 1 hour or until a meat thermometer inserted into thickest portion registers 150°F. Remove from grill, and let stand 10 minutes before serving.

Mac 'n Cheese with Bacon

1 pound elbow macaroni
4 cups milk
2 or 3 sprigs thyme
4 cloves garlic, crushed and
  divided
3 tablespoons unsalted butter
3 tablespoons flour
5 ½ cups shredded sharp white
  cheddar
Salt to taste
Black pepper, freshly ground
¼ cup chopped flat-leaf parsley
4 slices bacon, cut crosswise
  into thin strips
1 large onion, diced
2 garlic cloves, crushed
Fresh thyme

Bring a pot of salted water to a boil over high heat. Add the macaroni and cook for 8 to 9 minutes, until al dente. Drain.

Preheat the oven to 400°F. In a small saucepan, heat the milk with the thyme sprigs and 2 garlic cloves.

Melt butter in a large, deep skillet over medium-high heat. Whisk in the flour and cook for about 1 minute, stirring constantly to prevent lumps from forming. Strain the herbs from the milk and very slowly add milk to butter-flour mixture, whisking vigorously to prevent lumps from forming. Cook until mixture is very smooth. Stir in 4 cups of cheese and continue to cook and stir to melt the cheese. Season with salt and pepper. Add the cooked macaroni and parsley and fold in to coat macaroni with the cheese mixture.

Spoon into a greased 3-quart baking dish and sprinkle with the remaining 1 ½ cups cheese. Bake for 30 minutes, or until hot and bubbly.

While that bakes, heat a skillet. Add the bacon and cook until crispy. Pour off grease and add onion, garlic and thyme leaves and cook for about 5 minutes to soften the onion. Season with salt and pepper. Toss the bacon mixture over the macaroni and cheese. When serving, be sure to include the bacon on each spoonful.

Chicken

Chicken Fajitas

7 (½ inch thick) chicken cutlets
3 tablespoons fresh lime juice
2 tablespoons olive oil
1 teaspoon minced garlic
½ teaspoon ground cumin,
   oregano, and salt
¼ teaspoon pepper
2 tablespoons olive oil
4 medium onions, cut long
   ways into thin strips
3 large (red and green)
   peppers, cut into long strips

8 flour tortillas, stacked and
   wrapped in foil

Mix chicken and marinade ingredients: lime juice, olive oil, garlic and spices in a large resealable bag, shake, and set aside for 30 minutes.

Heat oil in a large Dutch oven or deep skillet; then add onions and cook on medium-high heat for 3 minutes. Add peppers and stir-fry for 2 minutes, then reduce heat. Add chicken and cook until done, turning only once (7 minutes on each side).

Mushroom Chicken Strips

3 to 4 chicken breasts,
   cut into strips
¼ cup (½ stick) butter or
   margarine
1 (4 ounce) can sliced
   mushrooms
1 (10.75 ounce) can cream
   of chicken soup
⅔ cup milk
Dash of garlic powder
Dash of poultry seasoning

Brown chicken in butter, add mushrooms, stir in soup, milk and seasonings. Cover and simmer until done.

Chicken Rice Bake

3 to 4 chicken breasts, cut into
   cubes
1 box Uncle Ben's brown wild
   rice
½ (1 ounce) package dry
   onion soup
1 (10.75 ounce) can mushroom
   soup
1 (10.75 ounce) can cream
   of celery soup
1 cup chicken broth
1 cup water

Mix all ingredients and pour into a greased 9 x 13-inch pan. Bake at 300°F for 50 to 60 minutes.

Chicken Enchiladas

1 pound chicken,
   cooked and shredded
2 (10.75 ounce) cans cream
   of chicken soup
1 (16 ounce) container sour
   cream
2 (10.75 ounce) cans green
   chilies (chopped)
2 (8 ounce) packages
   Monterrey Jack cheese
1 (16 ounce) package flour
   tortilla shells

Cook chicken and cut into shredded pieces. Mix all ingredients with chicken, using ½ package cheese. Spray 9 x 13-inch pan with cooking spray. Spread small amount of chicken mixture in bottom of pan and then fill shells with mixture. Top with remaining mixture and cheese. Cover and bake at 350°F for 45 to 60 minutes.

Chicken with Eggplant and Veggies

8 chicken legs with thighs

6 tablespoons olive oil
3 cups slivered onion
6 large cloves of garlic, minced
1 tablespoon sweet Hungarian
    paprika
1 tablespoon coarse (kosher)
    salt
1 teaspoon turmeric
1 teaspoon ground coriander
1 teaspoon fennel seeds
½ teaspoon ground ginger
Freshly ground black pepper
2 cups diced canned tomatoes,
    drained
1 cup water
3 tablespoons lemon juice
1 large eggplant, cut into
    1-inch cubes
2 tablespoons fresh flat-leaf
    parsley, chopped
Salt and pepper to taste

Prepare chicken by separating legs and thighs and remove skin.

Heat tablespoon of oil in a large Dutch-oven pan over low heat. Cook the onions and garlic, covered, until softened, 10 to 15 minutes, stirring occasionally. Add all the spices and stir over low heat for 1 minute to mellow the flavors.

Add the tomatoes, water, and lemon juice; bring the sauce to a boil for 2 minutes. Arrange chicken pieces in a single layer in the pan, spooning some sauce over them. Bring to a boil, reduce heat to medium-low, partially cover and simmer for 15 minutes. Turn chicken over and simmer until tender, about 20 minutes.

Meanwhile, preheat oven to 400°F. Toss eggplant with the remaining 4 tablespoons of oil. Spread on a baking sheet in a single layer and roast until soft and golden, about 25 minutes, tossing once. Put the eggplant and parsley on top of the chicken and serve.

Leftover Rotisserie Chicken and Extra Shrimp

Rotisserie chicken, shredded
Chicken ramen soup, spicy
Scallions
Hot sauce
Pizza crust
Prepared salsa
Cooked shrimp
Chili powder
Mexican cheese blend

Shred chicken. Prepare ramen noodle soup. Stir in shredded rotisserie chicken, sliced scallions and hot sauce to taste. Spread pizza crust with prepared salsa; top with chicken mixture and scatter cooked shrimp over top. Sprinkle with little chili powder and shredded Mexican cheese blend. Bake at 450°F for 10 minutes.

Texas Chicken Picante

1 ½ cups picante sauce
3 tablespoons light brown
   sugar
1 tablespoon mustard
4 chicken breast halves,
   skinless and boneless
3 cups hot cooked rice

Mix picante sauce, sugar, and mustard. Place chicken in 2-quart shallow baking dish. Pour picante sauce mixture over chicken. Bake at 400°F for 20 minutes or until chicken is done. Serve over hot cooked rice.

Chinese Chicken

1 pound chicken, boneless,
   skinless, and cut into strips
1 tablespoon oil
1 (6 ounce) package snow
   peas, trimmed
1 small red pepper,
   cut into strips
1 (3 ounce) package lemon
   flavor gelatin
1 tablespoon cornstarch
½ cup chicken broth
2 tablespoons zesty Italian
   dressing
2 cloves garlic, minced

Heat oil in large skillet and add chicken. Cook 4 minutes or until cooked. Add snow peas and peppers; cook and stir 2 minutes. Mix dry gelatin and cornstarch. To this add broth, dressing, and garlic and stir until dissolved. Add to skillet; reduce heat to medium and cook 3 minutes or until sauce is thickened.

Crispy Oven-Fried Tortilla Chip-Crusted Chicken

1 pound chicken breast tenders
½ teaspoon salt
¼ teaspoon pepper
⅓ cup flour
½ teaspoon dried oregano
½ teaspoon chili powder
¼ teaspoon ground cumin
2 large eggs
2 garlic cloves, pressed
Vegetable cooking spray
2 cups crushed tortilla chips
Pineapple-kiwi salsa
    (see page 125)

Preheat oven to 425°F. Sprinkle chicken with salt and pepper. In a plastic bag, add flour and next 3 ingredients. In a medium bowl, whisk eggs just until foamy and stir in pressed garlic. Crush chips in another plastic bag.

Place a wire rack coated with cooking spray in a 15 x 10-inch jelly roll pan. Dredge chicken tenders in flour mixture, shaking off excess; dip in egg mixture, and dredge in crushed tortilla chips. Lightly coat chicken on each side with cooking spray; arrange chicken on wire rack. Bake at 425°F for 18 to 20 minutes or until golden brown and done, turning once after 12 minutes. Serve with pineapple/kiwi salsa.

Fish

Creole Baked Fish

2 (12 ounce) packages frozen cod fillets, thawed according to package directions
½ red bell pepper, chopped
½ green bell pepper, chopped
1 small onion, chopped
1 tablespoon olive oil
2 garlic cloves, chopped
¼ cup dry white wine
1 (28 ounce) can diced tomatoes
1 tablespoon Cajun seasoning, divided
½ teaspoon pepper
2 teaspoons hot sauce

Preheat oven to 350°F. Sauté bell peppers and onion in hot oil in an oven proof skillet over medium heat 5 minutes or until tender. Add garlic and sauté for another minute. Add wine, and cook 3 minutes or until liquid is absorbed. Stir in tomatoes, 1 teaspoon Cajun seasoning, pepper, and if desired, hot sauce. Cook, stirring occasionally, for 10 minutes, then remove from heat. Sprinkle 1 side of cod fillets evenly with remaining Cajun seasoning. Place fillets, seasoned sides up, on top of tomato mixture in skillet. Bake at 350°F for 25 minutes or until fish flakes with a fork.

Mustard and Soy-Glazed Salmon

2 (12 ounce) packages frozen
    salmon fillets
¼ cup pepper jelly
¼ cup soy sauce
2 tablespoons country-style
    Dijon mustard
¼ teaspoon pepper

Bring pepper jelly, soy sauce, and Dijon mustard to a boil in a small saucepan over medium heat; reduce heat to low and simmer 5 minutes; add pepper. Remove from heat.

Place salmon fillets on a greased wire rack on an aluminum foil-lined baking sheet. Sprinkle fillets with half of pepper jelly mixture. Broil fillets 5 inches from heat 8 to 10 minutes or to desired degree of doneness. Remove from oven, and brush with remaining pepper jelly mixture.

Lemon-Dill Tilapia

4 (5 ounce) fresh tilapia fillets
1 teaspoon salt
½ teaspoon pepper
2 lemons, sliced
¼ cup shredded carrots
2 tablespoons fresh dill
2 tablespoons fresh parsley
2 tablespoons butter
Parchment paper

Preheat oven to 375°F. Sprinkle fillets with salt and pepper. Cut parchment into 4 (9 x 13-inch) rectangles. Place 3 lemon slices crosswise in center of 1 parchment rectangle. Top with 1 fillet. Repeat with remaining lemon slices, fillets, and parchment paper rectangles. Sprinkle fillets evenly with carrots, dill, and parsley. Top each fillet with ½ tablespoon butter. Fold 1 side parchment paper over fillet; tuck excess parchment under fillets, pressing folds to form a crease. Place on baking sheet and bake at 375°F for 20 to 25 minutes or until the fish flakes with a fork.

Crab-Stuffed Trout

2 (6 ounce) whole trout, cleaned and boned
3 teaspoons reduced-sodium soy sauce, divided
3 ounces cooked crab meat, shredded
2 slices bread made into bread crumbs
½ cup carrots, thinly sliced
¼ cup celery, thinly sliced
¼ cup green onion, thinly sliced
1 egg white, slightly beaten
1 tablespoon lemon peel, grated
1 teaspoon garlic powder
½ teaspoon ground black pepper

Preheat oven to 375°F. Wash trout and pat dry with paper towels. Place on foil-lined baking sheet. Brush inside cavities lightly with half of the soy sauce. Combine remaining soy sauce, crab meat, bread crumbs, carrots, celery, onion, egg white, lemon peel, garlic powder, and pepper in a small bowl. Place half the stuffing inside each trout. Bake 30 minutes.

Crab Casserole

1 can crab meat*
6 diced hard cooked eggs
1 cup mayonnaise
1 onion, diced
¼ cup parsley
⅔ cup half-and-half
Fresh soft bread crumbs
¼ cup green sliced olives

Mix together all ingredients except bread crumbs and olives. Pour into lightly greased casserole dish. Top with fresh buttered bread crumbs and decorate with olives. Bake at 350°F for 20 to 25 minutes until hot and bubbly.

*You can substitute shrimp or chicken for crab.

Vegetarian

Vegetable Combo Casserole

1 medium potato, peeled and
  cut into ½ inch pieces
1 medium yam, peeled and cut
  into ½ inch pieces
1 red bell pepper, seeded and
  cut into ½ inch pieces
2 carrots, peeled and cut into
  ½ inch pieces
5 tablespoons olive oil
1 red onion, thinly sliced into
  rings
2 small or 1 large zucchini, cut
  crosswise into ¼ inch pieces
Salt and pepper
2 large ripe tomatoes, cut
  crosswise into ¼ inch thick
  slices
½ cup grated Parmesan
  cheese
2 tablespoons dried
  Italian-style bread crumbs
Fresh basil sprigs for garnish

Preheat the oven to 400°F. Toss the potato, yam, bell pepper, carrots, and 2 tablespoons of olive oil in a 9 x 13-inch baking dish to coat. Sprinkle with salt and pepper and toss until coated. Spread vegetables evenly over the bottom of the pan. Arrange the onion slices evenly over the vegetable mixture. Arrange the zucchini over the onion. Drizzle with 2 tablespoons oil. Sprinkle with salt and pepper. Arrange the tomato slices over the zucchini. Stir the Parmesan cheese and bread crumbs in a small bowl to blend. Sprinkle the Parmesan bread crumbs over the vegetables. Drizzle with the last tablespoon of olive oil. Bake uncovered until the vegetables are tender, and the topping is golden brown, about 40 minutes.

Veggie Pizza

2 packages crescent rolls
1 (8 ounce) package cream
   cheese, softened
½ cup sour cream
2 tablespoon Hellmann's
   mayonnaise
1 package Hidden Valley
   Ranch dressing (original)
Assorted vegetables such
   as green peppers, yellow
   peppers, red peppers, green
   onion, celery, carrots,
   mushrooms, tomatoes,
   cauliflower, radishes
Cheese and bacon bits,
   if desired

Press crescent rolls flat on a cookie sheet or round pizza pan. Bake as directed on can or 10-12 minutes. Mix together cream cheese, sour cream, mayonnaise, and Hidden Valley Ranch dressing. Spread mixture over baked crescent rolls. Add assorted vegetables as toppings.

Two-Cheese Macaroni Casserole

¼ cup butter, cubed
2 ½ cups water
4 cups (16 ounces) shredded
   cheddar cheese
2 cups uncooked elbow
   macaroni
1 (8 ounce) container
   small-curd cottage cheese
⅛ teaspoon pepper
Pinch salt

In a large saucepan, bring water and butter to a boil. Remove from the heat; carefully stir in remaining ingredients. Transfer to a greased 2-quart baking dish. Cover and bake at 350°F for 45 minutes. Uncover; bake 10 minutes longer or until bubbly and macaroni is tender.

Valentino's Pizza Taste-Alike

Crust
1 cup warm water
1 package (2 ¼ teaspoons)
    active dry yeast
2 teaspoons granulated sugar

Add the following:
2 tablespoons olive oil
2 teaspoons salt
3 cups bread flour (more or
    less, depending on humidity)

Sauce
1 (6 ounce) can tomato paste
1 (8 ounce) can tomato sauce
¼ teaspoon oregano
¼ teaspoon thyme
¼ teaspoon rosemary
1 garlic clove

1 (8 ounce) package Monterey
    Jack cheese and Mozzarella
    cheese

In a large mixing bowl, stir yeast and sugar into warm water. Let sit for 5-10 minutes or until bubbles form and mixture starts to foam. Pour in olive oil, salt and half the flour and mix. Once this flour is incorporated, start adding more flour gradually until it is slightly tacky but doesn't stick to hands. Knead for 6 minutes until the dough is smooth and easy to work with. Lightly grease the bowl, cover with plastic wrap and let rise 1 to 2 hours.

Prepare and simmer sauce.

Roll, toss, or pat out the dough for crust on greased sheet. Brush with olive oil. Bake for 5 minutes at 425°F, then add sauce. Add desired toppings and cover with Monterey Jack and Mozzarella cheese or cheese of your choice. Bake at 425°F for 10 to15 minutes.

Portobello Mushroom Lasagna

¾ pounds dried lasagna
   noodles
Good quality olive oil
4 cups whole milk
12 tablespoons (1 ½ sticks)
   unsalted butter, divided
½ cup flour
1 teaspoon freshly ground
   black pepper
1 teaspoon ground nutmeg
1 ½ pounds Portobello
   mushrooms
1 cup freshly ground
   Parmesan cheese
Kosher salt

Preheat oven to 375°F. Bring a large pot of water to a boil with 1 tablespoon salt and a splash of oil. Add the lasagna noodles and cook for 10 minutes, stirring occasionally. Drain and set aside.

For the white sauce, bring the milk to a simmer in a saucepan. Set aside. Melt 8 tablespoons (1 stick) of butter in a large saucepan. Add the flour and cook for 1 minute over low heat, stirring constantly with a wooden spoon. While stirring, pour the hot milk into the butter-flour mixture. Add 1 tablespoon salt, the pepper and nutmeg, and cook over medium-low heat, stirring first with a wooden spoon and then with a whisk for 3 to 5 minutes until thick. Take off the heat.

Clean mushrooms and pat dry. Separate the mushroom stems from the caps and discard the stems or use for another purpose. Slice the caps ¼ inch thick. Heat 2 tablespoons of oil and 2 tablespoons of the butter in a large sauté pan. When the butter melts, add half the mushrooms, sprinkle with salt, and cook over medium heat about 5 minutes, or until the mushrooms are tender and they release some of their juices. If they become too dry add a little more oil. Toss occasionally to make sure the mushrooms cook evenly. Repeat with the remaining mushrooms and set all the mushrooms aside.

To assemble the lasagna, spread some of the sauce in the bottom of an 8 x 12 x 2-inch baking dish. Arrange a layer of noodles on top, then more sauce, then ⅓ of the mushrooms, and ¼ cup grated Parmesan cheese. Repeat 2 more layers of noodles and sauce, and sprinkle with the remaining Parmesan. Bake the lasagna for 45 minutes, or until the top is browned, and the sauce is bubbly and hot. Allow to sit at room temperature for 15 minutes and then serve.

Breakfast

Backyard Breakfast on the Grill

6 individual dinner-roll balls of frozen dough, (3 pound package) thawed
Olive oil and salt
6 eggs
6 slices Canadian bacon
Chopped fresh herbs (thyme, basil, oregano, tarragon, rosemary)
6 slices cheese (Provolone)
6 slices tomato
Roll out dough into 3 ½ inch rounds. Put olive oil on both sides and let bread dough rise until it becomes puffy.

Prepare charcoal grill and while grill is heating, grease a muffin pan and then crack eggs into the cups of muffin pans, and cover with foil. Place the pan on the grill and cook for 4 to 5 minutes and then set aside. Place Canadian bacon on sides of grill to warm, then place prepared bread rounds on grill, and cook until bottom is nicely browned. Flip bread over and quickly scatter herbs on top of each round, then top with cheese of your choice.

Place bread rounds on serving platter. Layer each with slice of tomato and Canadian bacon. Using a spoon, scoop out each egg and place on top of the Canadian bacon; then sprinkle each with snipped chives and a grinding of black pepper and serve.

Overnight French Toast Casserole

1 pound loaf French bread,
   sliced
4 ounces cream cheese,
   softened
½ pound bacon
8 eggs
1 ½ cups milk
1 cup heavy cream
Juice of one orange
2 tablespoons orange zest
½ cup (1 stick) butter, melted
1 teaspoon ground cinnamon
Powdered sugar
Orange slices

Slice bacon into small pieces and fry in skillet until crisp. Let drain on paper towel. Spread slices of bread with softened cream cheese. Place them face up in a buttered 9 x 13-inch baking pan. Sprinkle crisp bacon over them and top with another slice that has been spread with cream cheese, face up.

Beat eggs until foamy; add milk, cream, orange juice and zest, and melted butter. Sprinkle in cinnamon and beat. Pour slowly over bread slices. Make sure all layers of bread are soaking in the milk mixture by pressing down with a spatula. Cover with plastic wrap and refrigerate overnight.

When ready to bake casserole, remove plastic wrap and preheat oven to 325°F . Bake for 60 to 90 minutes or until middle is set. Dust with powdered sugar. Garnish with orange slices and serve with warm maple syrup.

CAKES AND PIES

Lemon-Cream Cheese Frosting
Luscious Tropical Dream Cake
Mayonnaise Cake
Mexican Fruit Cake
Oatmeal Cake
Pumpkin Cheese Cake
Rita's Sweet Crumb Cake
Sour Cream Coffee Cake
Strawberry Cake

Cakes and Frostings

Angel Food Cake
Apple Brunch Cake
Apple Walnut Cake
Banana Cake
Black Bottom Cupcakes
Carrot Cake
Carrot Layer Cake
Chocolate-Key Lime Cake
Coconut Cloud Cake
Cream Cheese Frosting
Earthquake Cake
Fluffy Meringue Frosting
Frosted Mayonnaise Cake
Fruity Angel Layer Cake
Heavenly Angel Food Cake
Icebox Fruity Cheesecake
Jamie's Coconut Cake
Lemon Rose Bundt Cakes

Pies

Pie Crust for Double Pie Crust
Pie Crust for Six Single Crusts
Berry-Apple Fantasy Pie
Candy Bar Pie
Creamy Coconut Pie
Gluten Free Flaky Pie Crust
Mississippi Mud Pie
Pecan Apple Pie
Pineapple Meringue Pie
Upside-Down Apple Skillet Pie

— Cakes and Frostings —

Angel Food Cake

1 ¼ cups sifted cake flour
½ cup granulated sugar, sifted
12 egg whites
1 ¼ teaspoons cream of tartar
¼ teaspoon salt
1 teaspoon vanilla extract
¼ teaspoon almond extract
½ teaspoon coconut extract
1 ⅓ cups sifted granulated
  sugar

Measure flour and ½ cup sugar. Sift 4 times. In large bowl, beat egg whites, cream of tartar, salt, and flavorings until soft peaks form. Add 1 ⅓ cups sifted sugar in 4 additions. Fold in flour mixture and pour in ungreased angel food cake pan.

Bake 375°F for 35 to 40 minutes. Cool upside down over a narrow-neck bottle.

Heavenly Angel Food Cake

2 ½ cups granulated sugar
1 ½ cups all-purpose flour
¼ teaspoon salt
2 ½ cups egg whites
1 teaspoon cream of tartar
1 teaspoon vanilla extract
1 teaspoon fresh lemon juice

Preheat oven to 375°F. Line bottom and sides of a 13 x 9-inch pan with aluminum foil, allowing 2 to 3 inches to extend over sides of pan. (Do not grease pan or foil.)

Sift together first 3 ingredients. Beat the egg whites and cream of tartar at high speed with a heavy-duty electric mixer until stiff peaks form. Gradually fold in sugar mixture, ⅓ cup at a time, folding just until blended after each addition. Fold in vanilla extract and lemon juice.

Spoon batter into prepared pan. Bake at 375°F on oven rack one-third up from bottom of oven. Bake for 30 to 35 minutes or until a wooden pick inserted in center of cake comes out clean. Invert cake onto a lightly greased wire rack, with pan over cake, until completely cool, 1 hour or more. Remove pan and peel foil from cake.

Transfer cake to a serving platter. Spread Lemon-Cream Cheese frosting evenly over top of cake.

Lemon-Cream Cheese Frosting

1 (8 ounce) package cream
   cheese, softened
¼ cup butter, softened
¼ cup fresh lemon juice
1 pound box powdered sugar
2 teaspoons lemon zest

Beat cream cheese and butter at medium speed with an electric mixer until creamy; add lemon juice, beating just until blended. Gradually add powdered sugar, beating at low speed until blended; stir in lemon zest.

Fruity Angel Layer Cake

2 lemons, divided
1 (1 pound) box angel food
　　cake mix
4 cups raspberries, divided
2 ½ cups blueberries, divided
¾ cup granulated sugar
3 tablespoons cornstarch
1 tablespoon butter
2 (8 ounce) containers frozen
　　whipped topping, thawed
¼ cup prepared lemon curd
　　(see recipe page 118)

Preheat oven to 375°F. Zest and juice
1 lemon. Prepare cake mix according
to package directions. Stir in 2 tablespoons lemon juice and 1 tablespoon
lemon zest. Divide batter evenly among
4 ungreased 9-inch cake pans. Bake 18
minutes, or until firm, and cool.

In saucepan, bring 2 cups each of raspberries and blueberries, and the sugar,
cornstarch, butter, and 1 tablespoon
water to a boil and cook for 1 minute.
Remove from heat and stir in 1 cup of
raspberries and 1 tablespoon each lemon juice and zest. Then spoon into bowl,
cover, and place in freezer for 5 minutes.

In separate bowl, combine whipped topping and lemon curd. Then place
1 cake layer on platter, top with ¾ cup
fruit mixture, leaving ½ inch border. Repeat with remaining cake layers and fruit
mixture. Coat top and sides of cake with
curd mixture. Slice remaining lemon and
use as garnish along bottom edges of
cake. Top with remaining berries.

Apple Walnut Cake

3 eggs
2 cups granulated sugar
½ cup vegetable oil
2 teaspoons vanilla extract
2 cups all-purpose flour
2 teaspoons baking soda
2 teaspoons ground cinnamon
½ teaspoon ground nutmeg
¼ teaspoon salt
4 cups diced unpeeled apples
1 cup coarsely chopped
   walnuts

In a mixing bowl, beat eggs, sugar, oil, and vanilla extract. Combine flour, baking soda, cinnamon, nutmeg, and salt and mix into the batter. Fold in apples and nuts. Spread into a greased 9 x 13-inch baking pan. Bake at 325°F for 50 to 60 minutes or until a toothpick inserted near the center comes out clean. Cool on wire rack.

Frost with cream cheese frosting.

Banana Cake

1 (2-layer size) yellow or white
   cake mix
1 teaspoon baking soda
1 cup cold water
2 eggs, beaten
3 ripe bananas
1 (3.4 ounce) package
   instant banana pudding
1 ¼ cups milk
1 (8 ounce) container
   whipped topping
Nuts, optional

Stir baking soda into cake mix. Add cold water and beaten eggs. Mix until smooth. Mash and fold in bananas. Pour into a greased and lightly floured 9 x 13-inch baking pan.

Bake at 350°F for 30 minutes.

Mix cold milk into banana pudding until thick and creamy. Fold in whipped topping. Spread over cake. Sprinkle with nuts, if desired.

Carrot Cake

3 small baby food jars pureed
  carrots
2 cups granulated sugar
1 cup oil
4 eggs, beaten
1 teaspoon vanilla extract
2 cups all-purpose flour
2 teaspoons baking powder
½ teaspoon baking soda
1 teaspoon ground cinnamon
½ teaspoon salt

In large bowl, mix together carrots, sugar, oil, and beaten eggs. Add vanilla. In another bowl, measure dry ingredients and gradually stir into carrot mixture. Pour batter into a greased and lightly floured 9 x 13-inch pan. Bake at 350°F for 30 minutes, then frost with cream cheese frosting.

Earthquake Cake

1 (2-layer size) German
  chocolate cake mix
1 cup nuts
1 ½ cups coconut
1 (16 ounce) box of powdered
  sugar
¼ cup (½ stick) melted butter
1 (8 ounce) package cream
  cheese, softened

Spray bottom and sides of cake pan. Add nuts and coconut on bottom. Prepare cake mix according to directions on box. Pour over the nuts and coconut. Stir together powdered sugar, melted butter, and cream cheese in a bowl. Then drop by spoonful on top of cake.

Bake at 350°F for 40 to 45 minutes. This is a very gooey dessert.

Carrot Layer Cake

2 cups granulated sugar
1 ¼ cups vegetable oil
4 eggs
2 cups all-purpose flour
2 teaspoons baking soda
2 teaspoons ground cinnamon
1 teaspoon salt
4 cups finely shredded carrots
1 cup raisins
1 cup chopped pecans

Filling

1 cup granulated sugar
2 tablespoons all-purpose flour
¼ teaspoon salt
1 cup whipping cream
½ cup (1 stick) butter or
   margarine
1 cup chopped pecans
1 teaspoon vanilla extract

Frosting

2 tablespoons butter or
   margarine, softened
2 (3 ounce) packages cream
   cheese, softened
3 cups powdered sugar
1 teaspoon vanilla extract

In large mixing bowl, beat sugar and oil together, then beat in eggs. Gradually add in flour, baking soda, cinnamon, and salt. Stir in carrots, raisins, and nuts. Pour into three greased and floured 9-inch round pans. Bake at 350°F for 35 to 40 minutes. Cool in pans 10 minutes and remove to wire rack. Cool completely.

Filling: In heavy saucepan, combine sugar, flour, and salt. Stir in cream and add butter. Cook and stir over medium heat until butter is melted and mixture comes to a boil, then reduce heat. Cook for 3 minutes, stirring constantly. Remove from heat; stir in pecans and vanilla extract. Cool. Then spread filling between cake layers.

Frosting: Stir together butter and cream cheese until smooth. Blend in vanilla extract. Gradually beat in powdered sugar until of spreading consistency. Frost sides and top of cake. Store frosted cake in refrigerator.

Jamie's Coconut Cake

1 cup (2 sticks) butter, softened
2 cups granulated sugar
4 large eggs
3 cups sifted self-rising flour
1 cup well-stirred canned
    coconut milk (NOT cream
    of coconut)
1 teaspoon vanilla extract

Coconut Filling
¾ cup granulated sugar
1 cup sour cream
4 tablespoons milk
½ cup sweetened flaked
    coconut plus ½ cup for
    sprinkling on cake

7-Minute Frosting
1 ½ cups granulated sugar
⅓ cup water
¼ teaspoon cream of tartar or
    1 tablespoon com syrup
⅛ teaspoon salt
2 large egg whites
½ teaspoon vanilla extract

Preheat oven to 350°F. Grease and flour three 9-inch round cake pans and set aside.

In large bowl, with mixer on medium speed, beat butter until creamy. Add sugar and continue beating 6 minutes or until light and fluffy. Add eggs, 1 at a time, beating well after each addition. Add flour and milk alternately to butter mixture, beginning and ending with flour. Add vanilla extract and beat until just mixed. Divide batter equally among prepared pans. Level batter in each pan by holding pan 3 or 4 inches above counter then dropping it flat onto counter several times to release air bubbles and produce more level cake layers.

Bake 25 to 30 minutes, or until toothpick inserted in center of layers comes out clean. Cool cake layers on wire racks 10 minutes. With small knife, loosen layers from sides of pans and invert onto work surface. While cake is baking, prepare coconut filling.

In medium bowl, stir together sugar, sour cream, milk, and ½ cup coconut until well blended. Using handle end of wooden spoon, poke holes in cake layers 1 inch apart, until each layer is poked all over. Spread ⅓ of filling on

Instructions continued on next page

each layer. Place first layer on cake plate, top with second then the third layer. Cover and refrigerate 1 hour or up to 3 days to absorb filling.

When ready to complete and serve cake, prepare 7-Minute Frosting.

In top of double boiler, or in medium stainless steel bowl with hand-held mixer on high speed, beat sugar, water, cream of tartar, salt, and egg whites for 1 minute. Place double boiler top or bowl over 1-inch simmering water, making sure water does not touch bottom of double boiler top or bowl. With mixer on high speed, beat sugar, water, cream of tartar or corn syrup, salt, and egg whites for 1 minute. Beat in vanilla extract. Frost top and sides of cake. Sprinkle cake with remaining coconut. Garnish with strawberries.

Tropical Dream Cake

1 (20 ounce) can crushed
   pineapple
1 (2-layer size) package yellow
   cake mix
1 ½ cups milk
1 (3.4 ounce) package instant
   lemon or vanilla pudding
2 cups whipped topping,
   thawed
½ cup coconut, toasted
½ cup chopped pecans

Drain pineapple, reserving 1 cup of juice; set pineapple aside.

Prepare cake batter as directed on package, substituting 1 cup reserved juice for 1 cup of the water.

Pour batter into greased 10 x 15-inch baking pan. Bake for 15 to 18 minutes or until wooden toothpick comes out clean. Cool.

Add milk to dry pudding mix. Beat with wire whisk 2 minutes or until well blended. Stir in drained pineapple. Spread over cake; cover with whipped topping. Sprinkle with coconut and pecans, then store in refrigerator.

Coconut Cloud Cake

4 cups plus 2 tablespoons
   sifted cake flour
1 ½ tablespoons baking
   powder
¾ teaspoon salt
¾ cup (1 ½ sticks) unsalted
   butter, softened
2 ¼ cups granulated sugar
2 ¼ teaspoons vanilla extract
6 large egg whites
1 ½ cups milk
Lemon curd
¾ cup sweetened flake coconut
   or 1 fresh ripe coconut

Fluffy Meringue Frosting
½ cup granulated sugar
½ cup corn syrup
2 large egg whites
⅛ teaspoon salt
1 ½ teaspoons vanilla extract

Preheat oven to 350°F. Lightly coat three 9-inch cake pans with softened butter or vegetable oil. Dust with flour and tap out any excess and set aside.

In a medium bowl, sift together the flour, baking powder, and salt and set aside. In a large bowl, using a mixer set at high speed, beat the butter and sugar until well combined. Add the vanilla and egg whites and continue to beat until light and fluffy. Reduce mixer speed to low and add half the flour mixture alternately with milk. Beat just until flour is completely absorbed. Add the remaining flour mixture and beat for 1 more minute. Divide the batter equally among all 3 cake pans and spread evenly.

Bake on medium rack of oven about 30 to 35 minutes, or until the tops spring back when lightly touched and a tester inserted into the center of each cake layer comes out clean. Cool in the pans on a wire rack for 15 minutes. Using a knife, loosen the cake layers from the side of the pans and invert the layers onto the wire rack to cool completely. Use a serrated knife to trim the mounded side of each layer to level them, if necessary.

Line the edge of a cake plate with

Instructions continued on next page.

3-inch wide strips of waxed or parchment paper and place a cake layer, trimmed side down, on the top. Spread the layer with ¾ cup lemon curd and place the second layer, trimmed side down, on top of the first. Spread another ¾ cup of lemon curd on the second layer and top with the last cake layer. Frost with Fluffy Meringue Frosting and serve at room temperature.

Frosting

In a double boiler over barely simmering water, combine all ingredients except vanilla extract. Using a hand-held mixture set at high speed, beat until the mixture is light and fluffy - about 6 minutes. Remove from heat and beat in vanilla extract. Beat 1 more minute until meringue forms stiff peaks.

Apple Brunch Cake

2 cups all-purpose flour
2 cups granulated sugar
½ teaspoon salt
1 teaspoon baking powder
2 teaspoons baking soda
2 teaspoons ground cinnamon
3 cups peeled and grated
    apples
1 ½ cups oil
4 eggs
½ cup walnuts
1 teaspoon vanilla extract

Frosting

1 (4 ounce) package cream
    cheese, softened
¼ cup (½ stick) butter, softened
½ teaspoon vanilla extract
½ pound powdered sugar
Milk, as needed for spreading
    consistency

In large mixing bowl, mix dry ingredients together with apples. Add oil, eggs, walnuts, and vanilla extract. Blend well. Pour in greased and floured Bundt cake pan.

Bake at 350°F for 50 minutes or until toothpick comes out clean. Cool cake 10 minutes before turning out. Allow to set overnight to age flavors.

Mix frosting ingredients until smooth. Drizzle frosting over cake.

Lemon Rose Bundt Cakes

2 (2-layer size) lemon cake mix
2 (3.4 ounce each) packages
   lemon pudding mix
   (not instant)
6 eggs
1 ¼ cups rose soda,
   commercial or home-made
⅔ cup oil

Glaze
1 (16 ounce) box powdered
   sugar
½ cup water
1 tablespoon rose syrup

Preheat oven to 350°F. Spray Bundt pan and mini Bundt pan with shortening or cooking spray, making sure all the creases of the fluted sides of pans are well greased.

By hand or in a mixer, combine cake mix, pudding mix, eggs and rose soda. Stir until well blended. Add oil and mix until smooth. Divide batter into prepared pans. Bake about 35 minutes for large cake and about 20 minutes for the mini cakes, or until tester inserted in the center comes out clean. Cool on wire rack.

For the glaze, combine powdered sugar, water, and rose syrup in a bowl. Whisk to form a smooth glaze. Pour glaze into a resealable plastic bag. Snip off a corner and drizzle glaze on cooled cakes.

Mayonnaise Cake

1 (2-layer size) chocolate cake
   mix (with pudding in the mix)
1 cup Hellmann's real
   mayonnaise
1 cup water
3 eggs

Grease and flour 2 layer cake pans or 9 x 13-inch pan. In a large bowl blend all ingredients for 30 seconds on low speed. Beat at medium speed for 2 minutes and pour into pan.

Bake at 350°F for 30 to 35 minutes or until cake springs back when touched in the middle. Cool in pans for 10 minutes and remove to cool on wire racks. Frost when cooled.

Frosted Mayonnaise Cake

¾ cup mayonnaise
1 cup granulated sugar
1 teaspoon vanilla extract
2 cups all-purpose flour
¼ cup baking cocoa
2 teaspoons baking soda
½ teaspoon salt
1 cup water

Chocolate Frosting
2 tablespoons butter, softened
1 ½ cups powdered sugar
2 tablespoons baking cocoa
2 tablespoons warm milk
1 teaspoon vanilla extract
Pinch of salt

Cream Cheese Frosting
½ cup (1 stick) butter, softened
1 (8 ounce) package cream
   cheese, softened
1 teaspoon vanilla extract
3 cups powdered sugar

In a large mixing bowl, beat the mayonnaise, sugar, and vanilla extract until smooth. Combine the flour, cocoa, baking soda, and salt; add to mayonnaise mixture alternately with water, beating well after each addition.

Pour into a greased 9-inch square baking pan and bake at 350°F for 25 to 30 minutes or until a toothpick inserted near the center comes out clean. Cool on a wire rack.

Frost with either Chocolate Frosting or Cream Cheese Frosting.

Chocolate frosting
In a small mixing bowl, beat butter until light and fluffy. Gradually beat in powdered sugar, cocoa, milk, vanilla extract, and salt. Frost cake and store in the refrigerator.

Cream cheese frosting
In a mixing bowl, beat butter, cream cheese, and vanilla extract until smooth, gradually beat in powdered sugar.

Mexican Fruit Cake

2 cups all-purpose flour
2 cups granulated sugar
2 teaspoons baking soda
2 eggs
1 (20 ounce) can crushed
    pineapple and juice
1 cup walnuts

Cream Cheese Frosting
1 (8 ounce) package cream
    cheese, softened
½ stick butter, softened
2 cups powdered sugar
1 teaspoon vanilla extract

Mix flour, sugar, and baking soda. In medium bowl, beat eggs; add pineapple and walnuts. Pour pineapple mixture into dry ingredients and beat until smooth. Then pour mixture into a greased 9 x 13-inch pan and bake at 350°F for 30 to 35 minutes. Let cool, and then frost with cream cheese frosting.

Beat cream cheese and butter until well blended. Gradually mix in powdered sugar and vanilla. Spread on cooled cake.

Oatmeal Cake

½ cup (1 stick) butter
1 cup oatmeal, quick or regular
1 ½ cups boiling water

1 cup brown sugar
1 cup granulated sugar
2 eggs, beaten

Sift together:
1 ½ cups all-purpose flour
1 teaspoon baking soda
1 teaspoon baking powder
¼ teaspoon nutmeg
¼ teaspoon salt

Topping
1 cup brown sugar
1 ½ cups coconut
3 tablespoons light cream
1 egg, unbeaten
1 cup (2 sticks) melted butter
1 cup English walnuts

Mix first three ingredients and let stand for 20 minutes, then add next three ingredients.

Combine all ingredients. Pour into a 9 x 13-inch pan. Bake at 350°F for 35 to 45 minutes.

Mix together topping ingredients and pour over hot cake. Place under broiler until lightly browned, approximately 2 minutes. Watch carefully!

Strawberry Cake

1 (2-layer size) white cake mix
1 (10 ounce) package frozen
  strawberries, thawed and
  pureed or 1 cup mashed
  fresh strawberries
1 (3 ounce) package
  strawberry gelatin
1 package mini marshmallows

Grease bottom and sides of two 9-inch cake pans or one 9 x 13-inch pan. Preheat oven to 350°F.

Prepare cake as directed on box. Mix strawberries and dry gelatin together.

Layer marshmallows on bottom of pan and pour cake mixture on top, and then put strawberries and gelatin on top of cake mixture.

Bake at 350°F for 35 to 40 minutes. Let cool and top with whipped topping.

Sour Cream Coffee Cake

Topping
⅓ cup brown sugar
¼ cup granulated sugar
1 teaspoon ground cinnamon
1 cup chopped nuts

Cake
½ cup (1 stick) butter, softened
1 cup granulated sugar
2 eggs
2 cups all-purpose flour
1 teaspoon baking soda
1 teaspoon baking powder
½ teaspoon salt
1 cup sour cream
1 teaspoon vanilla extract
Milk to thin the batter

For topping, mix all ingredients and set aside.

For cake: Preheat oven to 350°F. Generously grease a 9 x 13-inch pan.

In a large bowl, cream butter and sugar; add eggs. In a bowl or on wax paper, measure and add flour, baking powder, baking soda, and salt. Gradually add the dry ingredients to butter and sugar alternately with the sour cream, beginning and ending with flour. Mix in vanilla extract (may use milk to thin batter). Pour half of the batter into greased pan. Sprinkle ⅔ of topping on batter. Add remaining batter and sprinkle on remaining topping. Bake at 350° F for 30 to 35 minutes.

Rita's Sweet Crumb Cake

Cake
2 cups all-purpose flour
1 teaspoon baking powder
1 teaspoon baking soda
½ teaspoon salt
1 cup (2 sticks) butter, softened
1 cup sugar
2 large eggs
1 ½ teaspoons vanilla extract
1 cup sour cream
Powdered sugar
Milk

Filling
¼ cup granulated sugar
¼ cup brown sugar
1 teaspoon ground cinnamon
½ cup walnuts, chopped

Crumb Topping
¼ cup granulated sugar
¼ cup brown sugar
7 tablespoons flour
5 tablespoons butter, cut in
1 cup walnuts, chopped

Preheat oven to 350°F. Grease and flour a 9 x 13-inch pan.

In small bowl, prepare the Filling. In another bowl prepare the Crumb Topping.

In bowl or on wax paper, measure flour, baking powder, baking soda and salt. In bowl of electric mixer, cream the butter until smooth. Add the sugar gradually and continue beating until mixture is light and fluffy. Scrape the sides as needed. Add eggs one at a time and continue beating. Blend in the vanilla extract. Add dry ingredients to butter mixture alternately with sour cream, beginning and ending with flour. Mix until thoroughly combined. The batter will be thick.

Spoon half of the batter into prepared pan. Sprinkle Filling over batter. Top with remaining batter. Sprinkle on Crumb Topping. Bake for 45 minutes or until the cake is golden brown on top and begins to shrink away from sides of the pan.

In bowl, combine confectioners' sugar, milk, and ½ teaspoon vanilla. Drizzle icing over cake.

Black Bottom Cupcakes

1 (8 ounce) package cream
   cheese, softened
⅓ cup granulated sugar
1 egg, beaten
⅛ teaspoon salt
1 (6 ounce) package semi-
   sweet chocolate morsels
1 ½ cups all-purpose flour
1 teaspoon baking soda
½ teaspoon salt
1 cup granulated sugar
¼ cup cocoa
1 cup water
⅓ cup vegetable oil
1 teaspoon vinegar
1 teaspoon vanilla extract

Preheat oven to 350°F. Prepare muffin pans by greasing or inserting liners.

Combine cream cheese, ⅓ cup sugar, egg, and ⅛ teaspoon salt in a medium bowl; beat well until light and fluffy. Stir in chocolate morsels and set aside.

In another bowl, sift together flour, baking soda, ½ teaspoon salt, 1 cup sugar, and cocoa. Combine water, oil, vinegar, and vanilla extract; add to flour mixture. Beat at low speed until well blended. Fill muffin cups half full. Spoon 1 teaspoon cream cheese mixture into center of each cupcake.

Bake for 25 to 30 minutes. Let cool in pans 10 minutes. Remove from pans and let cool completely on wire rack.

Chocolate-Key Lime Cupcakes

1 (9 ounce) package
   chocolate wafer cookies
½ cup butter, melted
3 (8 ounce) packages cream
   cheese, softened
1 ½ cups granulated sugar
2 teaspoons key lime zest
⅓ cup fresh key lime juice
3 large eggs
12 jumbo-size aluminum
   foil baking cups

Preheat oven to 350°F. Place 12 jumbo-size aluminum foil baking cups in lightly greased muffin pans and coat with cooking spray.

Pulse chocolate wafer cookies in a food processor 8 to 10 times or until finely crushed. Mix together cookie crumbs and butter; firmly press on bottom and two-thirds up sides of each baking cup (about 3 tablespoons crumbs per cup). Beat cream cheese and sugar at medium speed with an electric mixer until blended. Add lime zest and lime juice, beating at low speed until well blended. Add eggs, 1 at a time, beating just until combined.

Spoon mixture into prepared cups, filling completely full. Bake for 20 minutes or until set. Cool in pans on wire racks for 15 minutes. Remove from pans to wire racks, and let cool 15 minutes or until completely cool. Chill for 4 hours.

Icebox Fruity Cheesecake

1 (8 ounce) package cream
   cheese, softened
1 cup powdered sugar
1 (8 ounce) container frozen
   whipped topping, thawed
1 teaspoon vanilla extract
1 butter cookie crust or pretzel
   crust, baked
4 cups assorted fresh berries,
   pitted cherries, or sliced fruit
½ cup seedless blackberry jam
¼ cup orange liqueur

Beat cream cheese and powdered sugar at medium speed with an electric mixer until blended. Fold in whipped topping and vanilla extract; spoon into prepared crust, cover, and chill for 8 hours.

Arrange fruit over cream cheese filling. Stir together jam and liqueur; drizzle over.

Pumpkin Cheese Cake

1 (8 ounce) package cream
   cheese, softened
¾ cup granulated sugar
3 tablespoons all-purpose flour
3 eggs
1 cup pumpkin
¼ teaspoon ground cinnamon,
   nutmeg, and ginger
Prepared graham cracker crust

1 cup sour cream
1 ½ tablespoons granulated
   sugar
½ teaspoon vanilla extract

Beat cream cheese and ¾ cup sugar and flour until smooth. Add eggs, pumpkin, and spices. Beat until well mixed. Pour into 9-inch graham cracker crust.

Bake at 350°F for 50 minutes or until set.

Combine sour cream and sugar with ½ teaspoon vanilla extract and spread over cheese cake and bake for 10 more minutes.

Pies

Pie Crust for 6 Single Crusts

4 cups pastry flour
1 teaspoon salt
2 cups Crisco shortening
1 cup carbonated lemon-lime
    beverage such as 7Up

Combine flour and salt. Cut in the shortening until fine and crumbly. Stir in 7Up. Divide dough in half, form into rounds, and wrap in plastic wrap. Refrigerate at least 30 minutes before rolling out.

This recipe makes 6 single crusts.

Pie Crust for Double Crust Pie

2 cups pastry flour
½ teaspoon salt
1 cup Crisco shortening
4 ounces carbonated
    lemon-lime beverage
    such as 7Up

Combine flour and salt. Cut in shortening until fine and crumbly. Add 7Up. Divide dough in half. Wrap in plastic wrap and refrigerator at least 30 minutes. Roll out to ⅛ inch thickness. Makes double crust.

Gluten Free Flaky Double Pie Crust

1 (8 ounce) package cream
    cheese, softened
12 tablespoons (1 ½ sticks)
    butter, softened
1 tablespoon sugar
½ teaspoon salt
1 cup rice flour
1 cup cornstarch
1 teaspoon xanthan gum

In a large bowl or mixer bowl, cream together the cream cheese and butter, sugar, and salt. Add flour, cornstarch, and xanthan gum.

Mix together with your hands until the dough comes together. Form into two balls, one larger for the pie bottom and smaller ball for top and flatten. Wrap in plastic and refrigerate at least 2 hours.

Roll out on bread board dusted with cornstarch. Dust top of dough lightly and roll it out for bottom and top crust.

Pecan Apple Pie

⅓ cup all-purpose flour
2 teaspoons ground cinnamon
¼ teaspoon salt
12 cups thinly sliced peeled tart
    apples (about 10 apples)
Pastry for double-crust 9-inch
    pie (See above for recipe)

Topping
1 cup packed brown sugar
½ cup all-purpose flour
¼ cup oatmeal, quick
½ cup (1 stick) cold butter
½ to 1 cup chopped pecans
½ cup caramel ice cream
    topping

Line two 9-inch pie plates with pastry. Trim and flute edges; set aside. In a large bowl, combine flour, cinnamon, and salt; add apples and toss to coat. Pour into pastry shells.

For the topping, combine brown sugar, flour, and oats; cut in butter until crumbly. Sprinkle over apples. Cover edges loosely with foil. Bake at 375° F for 25 minutes. Remove foil; bake 25 to 30 minutes longer or until filling is bubbly. When baked, sprinkle with pecans; drizzle with caramel topping. Cool on wire racks.

Creamy Coconut Pie

3 cups toasted coconut
¼ cup light brown sugar
⅓ cup melted butter
1 (14 ounce) can sweetened
    condensed milk
6 limes (zest 1 lime, juice
    of all 6)
¼ cup sour cream
1 (3.4 ounce) package instant
    white-chocolate pudding mix
1 (8 ounce) container frozen
    whipped topping, thawed

In a bowl, combine coconut, sugar, and butter until blended. Press into 9-inch pie plate.

Freeze.

In bowl, stir together condensed milk, 1 cup lime juice, 1 tablespoon lime zest and sour cream until blended.

Whisk in white-chocolate pudding mix for 1 minute. Let set 5 minutes. Fold in 2 cups whipped topping. Spoon mixture into frozen crust. Chill pie in refrigerator for 2 hours. Top with remaining whipped topping. Garnish with lime slices.

Berry-Apple Fantasy Pie

1 cup granulated sugar
4 teaspoons quick cooking
   tapioca
½ teaspoon ground cinnamon
2 cups fresh blackberries
2 cups sliced, peeled apples
2 tablespoons butter, cut up
Pastry for 9-inch pie

Prepare pastry for 2 crust pie (see recipes above) and divide in half. Form each half into a ball. On a lightly floured surface, roll one ball of the pastry into a 12-inch circle. Transfer the rolled-out pastry onto a 9-inch pie plate.

In large mixing bowl, stir together the sugar, tapioca, and cinnamon. Add the blackberries and apples slices. Toss gently till coated. Let stand for 15 minutes.

Spoon filling into pastry lined pie plate, then dot with butter. Trim pastry even with edge of the pie plate. Moisten the edge of the pastry with water.

On a lightly floured surface, roll out the remaining pastry into a 12-inch circle. Cut slits in the pastry to let steam escape. Place pastry on the filling. Trim the top crust to ½ inch beyond edge of pie plate. Fold top pastry and crimp edge. Cover edge of crust with foil to prevent over-browning.

Bake at 375°F for 25 minutes and remove the foil. Bake for 20 to 25 more, or until the crust is golden brown and the filling is bubbly. Cool on a wire rack.

Mississippi Mud Pie

Crumb Crust

1 ½ cups chocolate wafers, crumbled

¼ cup (½ stick) butter or margarine, melted

Filling

1 quart mocha or coffee ice cream

1 pint double chocolate ice cream

3 tablespoons coffee flavored liqueur

Chocolate Sauce

4 ounces unsweetened chocolate, broken into pieces

1 cup milk

½ cup granulated sugar

⅓ cup corn syrup

3 tablespoons butter or margarine

1 teaspoon vanilla extract

Combine crust ingredients until blended. Press crumbs on bottom and up sides of 9-inch pie pan. Freeze until firm.

In large bowl combine mocha ice cream and chocolate ice cream; let stand at room temperature about 15 minutes to soften. Stir in coffee flavored liqueur until well blended. Spoon ice cream mixture into frozen crust, smoothing the top, and return to freezer.

In a medium sauce pan over low heat, combine chocolate, milk, sugar, and corn syrup. Cook until chocolate is melted, stirring constantly. Remove from heat, stir in butter and vanilla extract. Pour warm sauce into a serving pitcher.

To decorate pie, top with whipped cream and grated chocolate. Serve with warm Chocolate Sauce. Serves 8 to 10.

Upside Down Apple Skillet Pie

2 cups apples, sliced
  (about 6 apples)
1 (12 ounce) can lemon-lime
  soda
½ cup (1 stick) butter
½ cup brown sugar
1 teaspoon ground cinnamon
1 (21-ounce) can apple pie
  filling
1 prepared pie crust
2 tablespoons apple juice or
  cider
1 tablespoon granulated sugar

Preheat oven to 425°F.

Peel and slice apples in lemon-lime soda. In a 10-inch cast iron skillet or oven-proof pan, melt butter over medium high heat. Stir in brown sugar and cinnamon. Cook until it begins to bubble - but do not let it burn. Drain apples and add to skillet. Cover with apple pie filling.

Place prepared pie crust over skillet. Tuck down edges of pie crust into the skillet with a wooden spoon. Brush top of pastry with apple juice and sprinkle with sugar. Cut slits in top of pastry to allow steam to escape. Place skillet on baking sheet. Bake in preheated oven for 30 to 35 minutes or until crust is golden brown. Remove from oven and let cool at least 1 hour before slicing.

Candy Bar Pie

3 (2.7 ounce) chocolate-
  coated caramel-peanut
  nougat bar
1 ½ (8 ounce) packages cream
  cheese, softened
½ cup granulated sugar
⅓ cup sour cream
⅓ cup creamy peanut butter
2 large eggs
⅔ cup semisweet chocolate
  morsels
2 tablespoons whipping cream
¼ cup coarsely chopped,
  lightly salted peanuts
1 pretzel crust

Pretzel Crust
2 cups finely crushed pretzel
  sticks (about 18 ounces)
¼ cup firmly packed light
  brown sugar
¾ cup melted butter

Preheat oven to 325°F.

Cut candy bars into ¼-inch pieces and arrange over bottom of pretzel crust. In medium bowl, beat cream cheese and sugar with an electric mixer until light and fluffy. Beat in sour cream and peanut butter. Add eggs, 1 at a time, beating until well combined. Spoon cream cheese mixture over candy in pie crust.

Bake at 325°F for 35 to 40 minutes or until set. Cool on wire rack 1 hour or until completely cool. Cover and chill 2 hours.

In a glass bowl, microwave chocolate and whipping cream until melted and smooth, stirring every15 seconds. Drizzle over top of cooled pie and sprinkle evenly with peanuts.

Crush pretzels in a food processor – keep them crunchy. Add sugar and butter and mix. Press into a lightly greased 9-inch pie plate.

Pineapple Meringue Pie

2 cups pecan shortbread
    cookie crumbs
1 ⅓ cups sweetened flaked
    coconut, divided
¼ cup butter, melted
2 cups milk
¼ cup cornstarch
3 large eggs, separated
1 cup granulated sugar, divided
1 (20 ounce) can crushed
    pineapple, drained
1 tablespoon butter
1 teaspoon vanilla extract

Preheat oven to 350°F. To prepare crust, mix together cookie crumbs, 1 cup coconut, and ¼ cup melted butter. Firmly press on bottom, up sides, and onto lip of a lightly greased 9 inch pie plate. Bake for 10 to 12 minutes or until lightly browned. Remove to a wire rack and let cool for 1 hour or until completely cool.

For the filling: whisk together milk and cornstarch in a heavy saucepan, whisking until cornstarch is dissolved. Whisk in egg yolks and ¾ cup sugar until blended. Cook over medium-low heat, stirring constantly until mixture comes to a bubble. Remove from heat. Stir in pineapple, 1 tablespoon butter, and vanilla extract. Immediately pour into cooled pie crust. Filling will thicken upon cooling.

For meringue: beat egg whites at high speed with an electric mixer until foamy. Add remaining ¼ cup sugar gradually, 1 tablespoon at a time, beating until stiff peaks form and sugar is dissolved. Spread meringue over hot filling, sealing edges. Sprinkle remaining ⅓ cup coconut over meringue. Bake at 350°F for 10 to 12 minutes or until golden brown. Watch carefully. Remove from oven to wire rack. Let cool for 1 hour or until completely cool. Refrigerate if not serving immediately.

COOKIES AND CANDY

Best Oatmeal Cookies
Best Sugar Cookies
Best-Ever Oatmeal Chip Cookies
Chocolate Covered Sugar Wafer
   Bars

Coconut Mounds
Colossal Oatmeal Cookies
Corn Flake Cookies
Crispy Chocolate Bars
Double Decker Cookies
Family Favorite Chocolate
   Chip Cookies
Kathy's Tumble Weeds
Mary B's Cookies
Microwave Peanut Brittle
Nutty Chocolate Fudge
Oatmeal Sandwich Cookies
Oatmeal Scotchies
Peanut Blossoms
Peanut Butter and Cereal Cookies
Peanut Butter Balls
Peanut Butter Cookies
Pumpkin Cookies
Scotcharoos
Ultimate Chocolate Chip Cookie

Drop Cookies

Ultimate Chocolate Chip Cookies

¾ cup butter-flavor shortening
1 ¼ cups firmly packed
    brown sugar
2 tablespoons milk
1 tablespoon vanilla extract
1 egg
1 ¾ cups all-purpose flour
1 teaspoon salt
¾ teaspoon baking soda
1 cup semi-sweet
    chocolate chips
1 cup large pecans

Heat oven to 375°F. In large bowl, add shortening and brown sugar and beat until creamy. Gradually beat in milk, vanilla extract, and egg. Combine flour, salt, and baking soda and mix into creamed mixture until just blended. Stir in chocolate chips and pecans. Drop rounded spoonful of dough about 3 inches apart onto an ungreased baking sheet and bake for 8 to 10 minutes for chewy cookies.

Family Favorite Chocolate Chip Cookies

2 ¼ cups all-purpose flour
1 teaspoon baking soda
1 teaspoon salt
1 cup (2 sticks) butter,
    softened, not melted
¾ cup granulated sugar
¾ cup brown sugar
1 teaspoon vanilla extract
2 eggs
1 (12 ounce) package
    chocolate chips

In a small bowl, measure flour, baking soda and salt. In a big mixing bowl, cream butter, sugar, and brown sugar. Beat in vanilla extract. Add eggs and beat. Gradually beat in the dry ingredients from small bowl, then add the chocolate chips. Bake at 375°F for 8 to 10 minutes.

Corn Flake Cookies

1 cup granulated sugar
1 cup corn syrup
1 teaspoon vanilla extract
¼ teaspoon salt
2 cups peanut butter
4 cups corn flakes

Heat first four ingredients in a saucepan over medium heat until boiling. Remove from heat and add peanut butter and mix until creamy. Add cornflakes; mix until well coated. Drop by spoonful onto wax paper. Let set until cool.

Mary B's Cookies

2 packages almond bark
1 cup peanut butter
1 cup peanuts
2 cups marshmallows
3 ½ cups Captain Crunch cereal

Melt almond bark; add peanut butter and stir until creamy. Add remaining ingredients and drop by spoonful onto waxed paper and let set up.

Best Oatmeal Cookies

1 ¼ cups (2½ sticks) butter or margarine
¾ cup firmly packed brown sugar
½ cup granulated sugar
1 egg
1 teaspoon vanilla extract
1½ cups all-purpose flour
1 teaspoon baking soda
1 teaspoon salt
1 teaspoon ground cinnamon
¼ teaspoon nutmeg
3 cups oatmeal, regular or quick

Heat oven to 375°F. Beat butter or margarine, sugars, eggs, and vanilla extract until creamy. Gradually add combined flour, baking soda, salt, cinnamon, and nutmeg; mix well. Stir in oatmeal. Drop by rounded tablespoonful onto ungreased cookie sheet and bake for 8 to 10 minutes.

Oatmeal Sandwich Cookies

1 cup oatmeal, regular or quick
3/4 cup granulated sugar
2 tablespoons all-purpose flour
1 teaspoon ground cardamom
¼ teaspoon baking powder
¼ teaspoon salt
1 egg, slightly beaten
½ cup (1 stick) butter, melted
1 teaspoon vanilla extract
1 cup slivered almonds
1 recipe Vanilla Cream (below)

Vanilla Cream

⅓ cup butter, softened
1 ¾ cups powdered sugar
1 teaspoon vanilla extract

Preheat oven to 325°F. Line a cookie sheet with parchment paper, or line cookie sheet with foil and lightly coat with nonstick cooking spray.

In a medium mixing bowl, combine oats, sugar, flour, cardamom, baking powder, and salt. In a small bowl whisk together the egg, butter, and vanilla extract until well combined. Add egg mixture to the flour mixture, stir until well combined. Add the almonds and stir until evenly distributed. Drop level teaspoons of dough 3-inches apart on prepared cookie sheet. Bake 10 to 12 minutes or until edges are brown. Let cookies cool completely then peel from parchment paper or foil. Repeat with the remaining dough.

For Vanilla Cream: In a medium mixing bowl beat together ⅓ cup softened butter with 1 cup powdered sugar until smooth. Beat in 1 teaspoon vanilla extract. Gradually beat in an additional ¾ cup powdered sugar until mixture is smooth and of spreading consistency.

For each sandwich cookie, spread bottom side of a cookie with a rounded teaspoon of Vanilla Cream. Place a cookie, top side up, on top of filling.

Best-Ever Oatmeal Chip Cookies

1 ¼ cups all-purpose flour
1 teaspoon baking soda
1 cup (2 sticks) butter or
  margarine, softened
1 cup granulated sugar
1 (3.5 ounce) package
  butterscotch instant pudding
2 eggs, beaten
3 ½ cups oatmeal, regular or
  quick
1 cup butterscotch or chocolate
  chips
½ cup English walnuts

Mix flour and baking soda and set aside. Combine butter or margarine, sugar, and dry pudding mix in a large bowl; beat until smooth and creamy. Beat in eggs. Gradually add flour mixture, then stir in oats (batter will be stiff). Stir in chips and nuts. Drop by rounded tea-spoonful onto ungreased baking sheet two inches apart. Bake at 350°F for 8 minutes.

Oatmeal Scotchies

1 cup (2 sticks) butter or
  margarine, softened
¾ cup granulated sugar
¾ cup firmly packed brown
  sugar
2 eggs
1 teaspoon vanilla extract
1 ¼ cups all-purpose flour
1 teaspoon baking soda
½ teaspoon salt
½ teaspoon ground cinnamon
3 cups oatmeal, quick
1 (12 ounce) package
  butterscotch chips

Heat oven to 375°F. Beat butter or mar-garine, sugars, eggs, and vanilla extract until creamy. Gradually add combined flour, baking soda, salt, and cinnamon; mixing well. Stir in remaining ingredi-ents. Drop by level tablespoonful onto ungreased cookie sheet. Bake for 8 to 10 minutes.

Colossal Oatmeal Cookies

½ cup (1 stick) butter or
   margarine, softened
1 ¼ cups granulated sugar
1 ¼ cups brown sugar
4 eggs
1 teaspoon vanilla extract
1 cup chunky peanut butter
2 ½ teaspoons baking soda
6 cups oatmeal, quick
1 (12 ounce) package
   chocolate chips
1 (12 ounce) package
   butterscotch chips
Also: M&Ms or other goodies

Preheat oven to 350°F. Cover baking sheets with parchment paper or aluminum foil.

In very large bowl, cream butter with the sugars. Add eggs one at a time and vanilla extract. Beat after each addition until fully combined. Stir in peanut butter. Mix in the baking soda, oatmeal, and chips. Drop by heaping tablespoons or small ice cream scoop on covered baking sheets. Dip bottom of cup in sugar and press to flatter only slightly. Bake for 8 to 10 minutes or until slightly brown. Do not overbake.

Peanut Blossoms

½ cup granulated sugar
½ cup brown sugar
½ cup shortening
1 egg
½ cup peanut butter
2 tablespoons milk
1 ¾ cups all-purpose flour
1 teaspoon baking soda
½ teaspoon salt
1 teaspoon vanilla extract
Granulated sugar for coating
Chocolate kisses

In a large bowl, cream sugars and shortening. Add egg and mix well. Blend in peanut butter and milk. Mix in dry ingredients and vanilla extract. Shape into 1-inch balls and roll in sugar. Place 2-inches apart on ungreased cookie sheet and bake at 350°F for 10 to 12 minutes until golden brown, then immediately top each with chocolate kiss.

Peanut Butter and Cereal Cookies

½ cup granulated sugar
½ cup corn syrup
1 cup peanut butter
2 cups rice crispy cereal

Bring sugar and syrup to a rolling boil. Remove from heat and add peanut butter. Stir until mixture is creamy. Add cereal and mix well. Drop by spoonful or roll into balls when cool enough to handle. Place on wax paper until they set.

Peanut Butter Balls

1 ⅓ cups creamy peanut butter
¾ cup (1½ stick) butter, melted
1 cup graham crackers, crushed
2 ¾ cups powdered sugar
1 (16 ounce) package white almond bark
1 (12 ounce) package semi-sweet chocolate chips

Cover cookie sheet with wax paper. In a large mixing bowl, combine peanut butter and melted butter until creamy. Add graham cracker crumbs and powdered sugar in small portions and mix thoroughly. Shape into balls and place on wax paper.

In a medium saucepan or double boiler, slowly melt almond bark and chocolate chips, stirring frequently. Dip formed peanut butter balls into melted mix and set on wax paper to dry.

Peanut Butter Cookies

1 (14 ounce) can sweetened
    condensed milk
¾ cup peanut butter
2 cups biscuit/baking mix
1 teaspoon vanilla extract
Granulated sugar for coating
Chocolate kisses

Beat sweetened condensed milk and peanut butter until smooth. Add biscuit/baking mix and vanilla extract and mix. Shape into 1-inch balls and roll in sugar. Place on ungreased baking sheet and bake at 375°F for 6 to 8 minutes or until lightly browned. Immediately top each with a chocolate kiss.

Tumble Weeds

1 (12 ounce) can salted
    peanuts
1 (7 ounce) can potato sticks
3 cups butterscotch chips
3 tablespoons peanut butter

Combine peanuts and potato sticks in a bowl and set aside. In a microwave safe bowl, heat butterscotch chips and peanut butter for 1 to 2 minutes or until melted, stirring every 30 seconds. Add to peanut/potato stick mixture and gently stir to coat evenly. Drop by rounded tablespoons onto wax paper lined baking sheets. Refrigerate until set; store in airtight container.

Pumpkin Cookies

1 cup granulated sugar
1 cup shortening
1 cup canned pumpkin
1 teaspoon vanilla extract
2 cups all-purpose flour
1 teaspoon baking soda
1 teaspoon baking powder
1 teaspoon ground cinnamon
Dash of salt
1 cup raisins

Cream together sugar and shortening. Add pumpkin and vanilla extract and mix. Sift together flour, soda, baking powder, cinnamon, and salt; gradually blend into creamed mixture. Add raisins. Drop by spoonful on an ungreased cookie sheet. Bake at 375°F for 10 minutes. Frost with powdered sugar frosting or cream cheese frosting, if desired.

Best Sugar Cookie

1 cup (2 sticks) butter
2 cups granulated sugar
2 eggs
1 cup oil
Pinch of salt
1 teaspoon vanilla extract
5 cups all-purpose flour
2 teaspoons baking soda
2 teaspoons cream of tartar
Granulated sugar for coating

Cream butter and sugar together. Add eggs, oil, salt and vanilla extract. Sift together dry ingredients and gradually add to butter and sugar mixture, then mix well. Shape into balls and roll in sugar, then flatten with a fork on a cookie sheet. Bake at 350°F for 10 minutes or until light brown.

Bar Cookies

Crispy Chocolate Bars

1 (6 ounce) package semi-
    sweet chocolate morsels
1 (6 ounce) package
    butterscotch morsels
½ cup peanut butter
5 cups corn flakes cereal

In a 3-quart saucepan, add chocolate, butterscotch morsels, and peanut butter. Stir over low heat until melted and smooth. Remove from heat. Add corn flakes. Stir gently until evenly coated. Using buttered spatula or waxed paper, press mixture evenly into 9 x 9-inch pan coated with cooking spray. Cut into squares when cool. Store in airtight container.

Double-Decker Cookies

⅔ cup butter, melted
1 (2-layer) yellow cake mix
1 egg
5 to 6 cups miniature
    marshmallows

Topping
1 (12 ounce) bag peanut
    butter chips
⅔ cup corn syrup
¼ cup butter
1 teaspoon vanilla extract
2 cups salted peanuts

Melt butter in a 9 x 13-inch pan. Mix cake mix, butter, and egg together in a bowl. Pat into pan. Bake at 250°F for 12 to 15 minutes. Remove from oven, sprinkle marshmallows over mixture and put back in oven to continue baking at 240°F for 5 to 7 minutes. Marshmallows will melt and be lightly browned. Let cool before adding topping.

In saucepan on stove top, combine peanut butter chips, syrup, butter, and vanilla extract until melted. Pour over cooled marshmallow layer. Top with salted peanuts.

Chocolate Covered Sugar Wafer Bars

1 (9 ounce) package of vanilla
   sugar wafers
1 (14 ounce) bag of caramels
¼ cup water
3 or 4 cups chopped peanuts
1 (8 ounce) Hershey chocolate
   bar, milk or dark

Separate the sugar wafers with a knife, carefully removing the filling, so that only the wafers remain. Place the empty wafers in stacks of 3. On a sheet of wax paper, take one wafer from each stack, and lay out on wax paper.

Put caramels in a microwave safe bowl and add the water. Melt caramels in the microwave, stopping after each minute to stir. (Alternately, melt caramels with water in double-boiler.) When completely melted, with a spoon, drizzle the caramel on each wafer, doing 5 at a time, and then put a second wafer from the stack on each. When you finish, drizzle caramel on all the remaining wafers on the wax paper the same way, 5 at a time. Drizzle caramel on all the ones you just finished, and add the third wafer to each of them. You should have 20 to 25 completed cookies with 3 wafers each and caramel in-between. Put the chopped peanuts in a bowl and using tongs, dip each cookie in the melted caramel, drain off the excess caramel, roll in the peanuts, completely covering the cookie and set on wax paper. Finish all the remaining cookies the same way. Let set for 10 minutes.

Break up the chocolate bar in a microwave safe bowl and microwave for 30 seconds at a time, stirring after each time, until it is completely melted. Using a spoon, drizzle the chocolate in stripes over the cookies. Let the cookies rest until completely set.

Scotcharoos

1 cup corn syrup
1 cup granulated sugar
1 cup peanut butter
6 cups rice crispy cereal
1 (6 ounce) package
   chocolate chips
1 (6 ounce) package
   butterscotch chips

Mix syrup and sugar. Bring to a slow boil and remove from heat. Add peanut butter and stir until creamy. Fold in cereal and pat in a greased 9 x 13-inch pan. Melt chips and pour over top of the bars.

Candy & Confections

Coconut Mounds

1 pound flaked coconut
3 cups chopped pecans
1 (14 ounce) can sweetened
   condensed milk
1 (16 ounce) bag chocolate
   chips
¼ pound paraffin

Mix coconut, pecans, and milk together in a large bowl. Chill for 30 minutes in refrigerator. Shape in small balls. Melt chocolate chips and paraffin in a double boiler. Dip balls in melted chocolate mixture and place on waxed paper to cool.

Nutty Chocolate Fudge

1 (7 ½ ounce) jar
   marshmallow cream
1½ cups granulated sugar
⅔ cup evaporated milk
¼ cup (½ stick) unsalted butter
¼ teaspoon salt
2 cups milk chocolate chips
1 cup semisweet chocolate
   chips
½ cup chopped nuts
1 teaspoon vanilla extract

Line an 8 x 8-inch baking pan with aluminum foil and set aside. Combine the marshmallow cream, sugar, evaporated milk, butter, and salt in a saucepan and bring to a boil over medium-high heat. Cook for 5 minutes, stirring occasionally. Remove from heat and add both kinds of chocolate chips and stir until mixture is smooth. Add nuts and vanilla extract and stir well to combine. Pour into the foil-lined pan. Refrigerate until firm, about 2 hours. Let stand at room temperature for 15 minutes before cutting into squares.

Microwave Peanut Brittle

1 cup raw peanuts
1 cup granulated sugar
½ cup corn syrup
⅛ teaspoon salt
1 teaspoon butter
1 teaspoon vanilla extract
1 teaspoon baking soda

In a 1 ½ quart glass bowl, stir peanuts, sugar, syrup, and salt together. Then microwave on high for 3 minutes. Stir and cook 3 more minutes on high. Stir in butter and vanilla extract and microwave for 2 more minutes on high. Mix in 1 teaspoon baking soda and stir quickly. Then spread on a buttered cookie sheet. When cool, break into pieces.

DESSERTS

Cake Brownies with Frosting
Caramel Apple Pastries
Cherry-Filled Crepes

Chocolate Caramel Dreams
Four-Layer Dessert
Heath Bar Candy Dessert
Cassie's Brownies
Lemon Curd
Oreo Balls
Pineapple Marshmallow Dessert
Strawberries and Cream Cheese
   Dessert
Strawberry Dessert
Strawberry Pretzel Dessert
Zesty Cherry Clafouti

Desserts

Caramel Apple Pastries

3 large baking apples, peeled,
    cored, and finely chopped
½ cup caramel sundae syrup
½ cup toffee bits
16 sheets phyllo pastry

Preheat oven to 375°F and spray baking sheet with cooking spray.

In mixing bowl, combine chopped apples, sundae syrup, and toffee bits; set aside. Unroll phyllo pastry sheets and lay them flat under a sheet of plastic wrap. Place a slightly damp kitchen towel over plastic. Remove one sheet of phyllo and cover completely with cooking spray. Top with another sheet of phyllo; spray with cooking spray. Repeat until four sheets of phyllo are stacked. Cut the stacked phyllo into 2 equal rectangles.

Spread ⅓ cup apple mixture 1-inch from a short edge of the dough. Fold in long edges about ½ inch, then roll, beginning with filled end, until a cylinder is formed. Repeat with remaining phyllo and filling. Place each roll on greased baking sheet. Spray tops of each roll with cooking spray. Bake 12 to 15 minutes or until golden brown. Let stand for 5 minutes and drizzle with more sundae syrup and serve with ice cream.

Oreo Balls

36 Oreo cookies, finely crushed (about 3 cups)
1 (8 ounce) package cream cheese

Almond bark

Crush Oreos and mix with cream cheese. Shape into 1-inch balls. Place in freezer for 15 minutes. While Oreo balls are cooling, melt almond bark. Dip balls in almond bark and let set on wax paper-lined baking sheet.

Cassie's Brownies

2 cups graham cracker crumbs
½ cup (1 stick) butter
1 (6 ounce) bag chocolate chips
1 (6 ounce) bag butterscotch chips
1 cup coconut
1 cup pecans
1 (14 ounce) can sweetened condensed milk

In 9 x 13-inch pan, melt butter. Sprinkle crumbs over butter, mix together and pat in pan. Top with chocolate and butterscotch chips, coconut, and pecans. Pour the condensed milk over all. Bake at 350°F for 20 to 25 minutes.

Cherry-Filled Crepes

Crepes
2 eggs
1 cup milk
½ teaspoon almond extract
½ cup cornstarch
½ cup all-purpose flour
1 tablespoon vegetable oil
2 teaspoons granulated sugar
¾ teaspoon baking powder
¼ teaspoon salt
Pinch ground allspice

Filling
⅔ cup pomegranate-cherry
   juice
1 tablespoon cornstarch
2 teaspoons granulated sugar
2 bags (10 ounce each) frozen,
   pitted sweet cherries or
   1 ¼ pound fresh sweet
   cherries, pitted

In medium-size bowl, whisk eggs, milk, and remaining ingredients. Refrigerate 20 minutes and stir.

Heat an 8-inch nonstick skillet over medium-high heat until hot. With ladle or ¼ cup measure, add 2 tablespoons batter to skillet, tilt, and rotate pan to coat the pan. Cook 30 seconds or until crepe is browned on bottom and dry on edges. Lift with a silicone spatula and flip over. Cook 5 seconds, and then transfer to a sheet of waxed paper.

Repeat with remaining batter for about 18 total, stacking crepes with waxed paper in between them. Crepes can be wrapped and frozen for up to 1 month.

For the filling: In a saucepan, blend juice, cornstarch, and granulated sugar. Cook over medium-high heat for 6 minutes or until thickened. Stir in cherries; heat 5 minutes. If too thin, combine 2 more teaspoons cornstarch and 1 tablespoon water. Stir into pan; cook until thickened. Place one crepe flat on a plate. Spoon about 2 tablespoon filling on one quarter. Fold crepe over, then fold again to form fan shape. Repeat with remaining crepes and drizzle with additional sauce.

Cake Brownies with Frosting

2 cups all-purpose flour
2 cups granulated sugar
1 teaspoon baking soda
1 cup (2 sticks) butter
1 cup water
3 tablespoons cocoa
½ cup buttermilk
2 eggs, beaten
1 teaspoon vanilla

Frosting

½ cup (1 stick) butter
3 tablespoons cocoa
6 tablespoons buttermilk
1 teaspoon vanilla
1 (1 pound) package
   powdered sugar (3 ½ cups)
1 cup English walnuts

Preheat oven to 350°F. Grease and flour large sheet cake pan.

In large mixing bowl, stir together the 3 dry ingredients and set aside.

In medium saucepan, add butter, water, and cocoa; stir and bring to a boil. Then pour mixture over dry ingredients. Mix and add buttermilk, beaten eggs, and vanilla. Mix well.

Bake for 15 to 20 minutes. Frost while still warm with frosting.

For frosting: In medium pan, add butter, cocoa, and buttermilk. Bring to a boil. Take off stove; add vanilla. Stir in powdered sugar and walnuts and pour over warm brownies.

4 Layer Dessert

1st Layer

1 cup all-purpose flour
1 stick (½ cup) butter or
   margarine
¾ cup chopped pecans

2nd Layer

1 (8 ounce) package cream
   cheese
1 cup powdered sugar
½ of a large (12 ounce)
   container whipped topping

3rd Layer

2 (3 ounce) packages instant
   pudding (any flavor)
3 cups milk

4th Layer

½ of a large container whipped
   topping
¼ cup pecan pieces

1st Layer: Mix and pat in 9 x 13-inch pan. Bake at 350°F for 20 minutes. Let cool.

2nd Layer: Mix well and spread over crust. Chill.

3rd Layer: Mix, spread, and chill.

4th Layer: Spread remaining whipped topping over pudding and chill. Top with pecan pieces.

Chocolate Caramel Dreams

2 cups chocolate wafer crumbs
⅓ cup butter, melted
½ cup caramel ice cream
   topping
30 vanilla caramels
¼ cup whipping cream
2 cups chopped pecans
¾ cup semisweet chocolate
   pieces
¼ cup whipping cream

In medium mixing bowl, stir together chocolate wafer crumbs and melted butter. Press onto the bottom of a 9-inch springform pan. Bake at 350°F for 10 minutes. Cool slightly on a wire rack.

In a heavy medium saucepan over low heat, melt caramel ice cream topping and caramels, stirring often. Stir in the first ¼ cup whipping cream. Remove from heat; stir in nuts. Spread over crust. Cool, cover, and chill for 1 hour.

For topping: In a heavy small saucepan or microwave, melt chocolate pieces. Remove from heat; stir in remaining ¼ cup whipping cream. Drizzle or spread over caramel-pecan mixture. Cover and chill for at least 1 hour.

Heath Bar Candy Dessert

1 cup all-purpose flour
¼ cup brown sugar
½ cup chopped nuts
½ cup (1 stick) butter, melted

1 (6 ounce) package instant
   vanilla instant pudding
2 cups cold milk
¼ teaspoon burnt sugar extract
½ teaspoon vanilla extract
1 cup softened butter-brickle
   ice cream

1 (8 ounce) container whipped
   topping
2 large Heath candy bars

Press into 9 x 13-inch pan and bake for 20 minutes at 350°F.

Beat second set of ingredients until smooth and pour over crust.

Spread whipped topping over pudding mix and sprinkle with crunched up candy bar. Chill for several hours.

Lemon Curd

4 large egg yolks
3 large eggs
¾ cup granulated sugar
½ cup (about 3 lemons) fresh
   lemon juice
2 tablespoons whole milk
1 tablespoon cornstarch
6 tablespoons unsalted butter,
   cut into ½ inch pieces

In medium size non-reactive saucepan, use a whisk to lightly beat the egg yolks and eggs. Stir in the sugar, lemon juice, milk, and cornstarch. Add the butter and place saucepan over medium-low heat. Cook, stirring constantly being sure to reach all sides and corners of the pan, until the mixture thickens (5 to 8 minutes). Do not allow the curd to boil. The resulting curd should have the consistency of a light pudding.

Cool the lemon curd in the saucepan for 5 minutes. Use a fine sieve to strain the cooled curd and refrigerate in an airtight container. Will keep up to 1 week.

Pineapple Marshmallow Dessert

1 (16 ounce) package large
   marshmallows
2 cups milk
1 (20 ounce) can crushed
   pineapple, drained
2 cups whipped topping
2 cups graham cracker crumbs
½ cup (1 stick) butter

Melt marshmallows with milk in a heavy saucepan over medium heat, being careful they don't burn. (Can use a double boiler instead of saucepan). Cool, stirring occasionally. Fold together pineapple and whipped topping and add after marshmallow mixture.

In a 9 x 13-inch pan, melt butter, then add graham cracker crumbs Take out ½ of crushed graham crackers and reserve. Spoon pineapple and marshmallow mixture over crumbs and then sprinkle the remaining crumbs on top. Refrigerate until set.

Strawberries and Cream Cheese Dessert

1 package (13 ounce) Pecan Sandies cookies, crushed
¼ cup (½ stick) butter or margarine, melted

Stir together cookies and butter and press into the bottom of a 9 x 13-inch pan. Bake at 375°F for 15 minutes or until lightly brown.

1 (8 ounce) package cream cheese, softened
1 (3 ounce) package cheesecake flavored pudding mix
¼ to ½ cup milk

Mix cream cheese and dry pudding mix. Add enough milk, stirring well for easy spreading consistency. Spread over crust.

2 quarts fresh strawberries, sliced
2 containers (tubs) of strawberry glaze

Stir together strawberries and glaze and pour over the cream cheese mixture.

1 (3 ounce) package cheese-cake flavored pudding mix
1 (16 ounce) container whipped topping, thawed

Mix together pudding and whipped topping and spread over the strawberries. Cover and refrigerate overnight or several hours.

Strawberry Dessert

1 (2-layer size) white cake mix (not pudding)
2 (3 ounce) packages of strawberry gelatin
1 (12 ounce) can strawberry soda pop
1 (3.4 ounce) package vanilla instant pudding
1 ½ cups milk
1 (8 ounce) container whipped topping

Bake cake according to directions. Cool and prick with a fork.

Prepare 2 packages gelatin dissolved in 1 cup boiling water. Add 1 can strawberry soda pop and pour over cake. Prepare instant vanilla pudding with 1 ½ cups milk. Add whipped topping, gently stir, and spoon over cake. Keep refrigerated.

Strawberry Pretzel Dessert

2 cups pretzel sticks, broken in small pieces
¾ cup (1 ½ sticks) butter, melted
3 tablespoons granulated sugar
1 (8 ounce) package cream cheese, softened
½ cup granulated sugar
1 (8 ounce) container whipped topping
2 (3 ounce) packages strawberry gelatin
2 cups boiling water
1 (8 ounce) can crushed pineapple
3 cups sliced strawberries

Combine pretzels with butter and sugar. Press lightly into a greased 9 x 13-inch pan. Bake at 350°F for 8 minutes and cool. Mix together cream cheese and sugar until creamy. Fold in whipped topping and spread on cooled crust; refrigerate until well cooled.

Dissolve gelatin in the boiling water. Cool slightly and add can of crushed pineapple with juice. Add strawberries just before gelatin begins to gel. Pour gelatin mixture over cream cheese and refrigerate until set, then spread more whipped topping over top. Refrigerate for several hours or overnight.

Zesty Cherry Clafouti

1 cup blueberries
1 cup pitted cherries, halved
2 eggs
½ cup milk
6 tablespoons granulated sugar
6 tablespoons all-purpose flour
2 tablespoons butter

Preheat oven to 375°F. Grease four (4 ounce each) ramekins and place on baking sheet. Divide blueberries and cherries evenly among ramekins.

In blender or food processor, combine eggs, milk, sugar, flour, and melted butter and process for 2 minutes or until smooth. Divide mixture evenly among ramekins.

Bake 15 minutes, or until tops puff (they will sink during cooling) and toothpick inserted in center comes out clean. Garnish each ramekin with dollop of whipped cream or scoop of ice cream and berries.

THIS 'N THAT

Chip Dip
Mexican Dip
Shrimp Dip
Hot Chopped Beef Dip
Dried Beef Ball
Big Mac Sauce
Soda Pop and Soy Marinade
French Dressing
Salsa
Pineapple-Kiwi Salsa

Chow-Chow
Refrigerator Pickles
Homemade Granola
Chex Muddy Buddies
Chex Party Mix
New Trail Mix
Butterscotch Coffee
Golden Punch
Mint Recipe

This 'n That

Chip Dip

2 pounds Velveeta cheese
1 can Ro-Tel tomatoes and
  chilies
1 pound hamburger or sausage

Melt cheese in double boiler or crock pot. Cook hamburger or sausage. Drain well. Add well-chopped tomatoes and chilies to cheese mixture and mix well. Add hamburger or sausage until mixed well into cheese sauce. Serve with potato chips or tortilla chips.

Mexican Dip

1 (8 ounce) package cream
  cheese
1 (8 ounce) container sour
  cream
1 cup bean dip
1 small jar picante sauce
Shredded lettuce
Chopped tomatoes
Cheddar cheese

Soften cream cheese. Mix cream cheese and sour cream. Spread in 9 x 9-inch pan, then layer the ingredients, beginning with bean dip, and adding in layers: picante sauce, lettuce, tomatoes, and cheese.

Shrimp Dip

1 cup tomato soup
1 envelope Knox gelatin
1 (8 ounce) package cream
  cheese
1 cup mayonnaise
1 onion, chopped
1 green pepper, chopped
2 (4 ounce) cans deveined
  shrimp

Heat tomato soup and add gelatin and cream cheese. Stir until creamy. Cool and add the remaining ingredients; stir until mixed. Refrigerate until ready to serve with crackers.

Hot Chopped Beef Dip

2 (8 ounce) packages cream
  cheese, softened
1 (8 ounce) container sour
  cream
2 tablespoons milk
1 tablespoon Worcestershire
  sauce

¼ cup minced onions
½ cup finely chopped green
  pepper
2 (3 ounce) packages chopped
  beef, finely chopped

Cream first four ingredients and add rest of ingredients.

Bake at 350°F for 30 minutes.

Dried Beef Ball

1 package dried beef
1 (8 ounce) package cream
  cheese, softened
1 jar pimento cheese
¼ cup mayonnaise
3 - 4 chopped green onions
Dash garlic salt

Mix half of the dried beef and remaining ingredients. Form into ball and roll in remaining beef.

Big Mac Sauce

1 cup Miracle Whip
⅓ cup creamy French dressing
¼ cup sweet pickle relish
1 tablespoon sugar
¼ teaspoon pepper
1 teaspoon dry minced onion

Combine ingredients and refrigerate. Makes 2 cups.

Soda Pop and Soy Marinade

1 cup lemon-lime soda
1 tablespoon light brown sugar
3 tablespoons soy sauce
2 tablespoons olive oil
1 tablespoon Worcestershire
    sauce
2 garlic cloves, pressed
¾ teaspoon ground ginger
⅛ teaspoon ground cloves

Whisk together lemon-lime soda and remaining ingredients until thoroughly blended. Use immediately.

French Dressing

¾ cup sugar
¾ teaspoon garlic powder
¾ teaspoon dry mustard
¾ teaspoon celery seed
⅛ teaspoon black pepper
1 teaspoon salt
⅓ cup salad oil
⅓ cup vinegar
1 (10.75 ounce) can tomato
    soup

Mix all together in a blender. Pour in a jar and refrigerate.

Salsa

8 pounds (about 32 medium) tomatoes, peeled and chopped
2 cups onion, chopped
2 cups celery, chopped
2 cups sugar
2 cups cider vinegar
½ cup canning salt
¼ cup mustard seed
8 red and green peppers, chopped
2 jalapeno peppers, no seeds

In large pan, combine all ingredients and boil for 30 minutes. To thicken, use 12 tablespoons corn starch.

Pineapple-Kiwi Salsa

2 (8 ounce) cans pineapple tidbits, drained
2 kiwi, peeled and diced
2 tablespoons fresh cilantro leaves, minced
2 tablespoons fresh lime juice
1 teaspoon minced jalapeno pepper

Stir together ingredients; add salt to taste.

Chow-Chow

1 gallon onions, chopped
1 gallon green tomatoes, chopped
1 gallon green peppers, chopped
½ gallon red peppers, chopped
1 head cabbage, chopped
1 large stalk celery, chopped
⅓ cup salt
10 cups cider vinegar
12 cups sugar
4 tablespoons celery seed
4 tablespoons mustard seed
Dash cinnamon
Dash mace
Dash ground cloves
2 tablespoons turmeric

Mix onions, tomatoes, peppers (red and green), cabbage, and celery with ⅓ cup salt. Let stand for 2 hours. Heat the vinegar and spices. While vinegar and spice are coming to a boil, squeeze vegetables as dry as you can. Then add to boiling vinegar. Bring back to a good boil and have canning jars ready and seal at once. You can cut this recipe in half.

Refrigerator Pickles

For dressing
1 ½ cups white vinegar
2 cups sugar
⅔ teaspoon tumeric
1 teaspoon mustard seed
1 teaspoon celery seed
Scant ¼ cup salt

Slice an ice cream bucket full of cucumbers and add 1 large onion, sliced.

Mix dressing for 5 minutes, and then pour over cucumbers and onions. Pickles will keep for 6 weeks in refrigerator.

Homemade Granola

18 ounces oatmeal, regular
4 cups Grape Nuts cereal
12 ounces whole natural almonds
16 ounces honey-roasted soy nuts
6 ounces dried cranberries
3 cups raisins
½ cup honey
½ cup dark brown sugar
8 ounces unsweetened applesauce

Combine honey, brown sugar and applesauce in a bowl and microwave until warm. Mix well. Mix in the oatmeal and let sit for a few minutes until oatmeal has absorbed the applesauce mixture. Add remaining ingredients and mix well. Store in airtight bags or containers in the refrigerator.

Chex Muddy Buddies

9 cups of your favorite Chex cereal
1 cup semi-sweet chocolate chips
½ cup peanut butter
¼ cup (½ stick) butter or margarine
1 teaspoon vanilla extract
1 ½ cups powdered sugar

Measure ingredients and pour cereal into large bowl and set aside. Combine chocolate chips, peanut butter, and butter in 1-quart microwave bowl. Microwave on high 1 to 1 ½ minutes or until smooth, stirring after 1 minute. Stir in vanilla. Pour chocolate mixture over cereal, stirring until all pieces are evenly coated. Pour cereal mixture into large resealable plastic bag with powdered sugar. Seal securely. Shake until all pieces are well coated. Spread on waxed paper to cool. Share it with your family and friends. If you happen to have leftovers, store in a resealable bag or airtight container.

Chex Party Mix

¼ cup (½ stick) butter
1 ¼ teaspoons seasoned salt
4 ½ teaspoons Worcestershire
  sauce
8 cups corn, rice, and/or wheat
  Chex cereal
1 cup mixed nuts
1 cup pretzels

In a microwave safe bowl melt butter on high and add seasoned salt and Worcestershire sauce; mix well. Pour cereals, nuts and pretzels into 2-gallon resealable plastic bag. Pour butter mixture over cereal mixture. Seal top of bag and shake until evenly coated. Pour contents of bag into big microwave safe bowl. Microwave on high 5-6 minutes; stirring every 2 minutes. Spread on wax paper to cool. Store in airtight bowl or container.

New Trail Mix

1 (14.5 ounce) package
  (or more) original Bugles
1 family size Gardetto
  pretzel mix
2 bags Ritz chips, plain
1 can cashews (or mixed nuts)
1 bag Gardetto rye chips
2 packages dry ranch mix

Mix all ingredients in a big bowl or roaster. Take 2 packages dry ranch dip mix and mix in with all the ingredients. Bake at 250°F for 1 hour, stirring every 15 minutes.

Butterscotch Coffee

1 cup butterscotch chips,
  divided
8 cups hot brewed coffee
½ cup half-and-half
5 to 8 tablespoons sugar
Whipped cream in a can

In a small microwave-safe bowl, heat ½ cup butterscotch chips at 70% power until melted, stirring occasionally. Cut a small hole in the corner of a pastry or plastic bag; insert a #4 round tip. Fill with melted chips. Pipe 8 garnishes onto a waxed paper-lined baking sheet. Refrigerate until set, about 10 minutes. In large pitcher, stir coffee and remaining butterscotch chips until chips are melted. Stir in cream and sugar. Pour into mugs. Top each serving with whipped cream and a butterscotch garnish.

Golden Punch

2 (12 ounce) cans frozen
  orange juice
2 (12 ounce) cans frozen
  lemonade
1 (46 ounce) can apricot nectar
4 (46 ounce) cans pineapple
  juice
3 quarts ginger ale
1 cup sugar

Combine all juices with sugar and mix well. Store in freezer until partly frozen. Put in punch bowl and add ginger ale.

Mint Recipe

1 (1 pound) box powdered
  sugar
1 (8 ounce) package cream
  cheese, softened
1 teaspoon extract or flavor of
  your choice

Mix together and set in refrigerator overnight until stiff. Put small amount in a bowl and put ½ cup granulated sugar in another bowl. Put sugar in mold and dump out excess before putting mints in. Roll into ball that fits the mold you're using. Roll in sugar and place on cookie sheet or waxed paper until firm. Can be frozen if making ahead of time.

About Nancy . . . .

Nancy Lantz says she is not a chef, just a foodie who likes to collect recipes and cook. Here she has compiled a collection of her favorite recipes as well as those volunteered from family and friends.

Nancy was born and grew up in northwest Missouri, an area blessed with an abundance of food 'fresh from the garden.' Many of the recipes here use foods readily grown in the Heartland. She said she wanted to share these so others could enjoy them as well.

A nurse by profession, Nancy has been employed by St. Francis Hospital, Maryville, Missouri, for forty years. She comments, "Although nursing has been my life, cooking is my pastime. My hope is that you will discover many of your own favorites in this collection."

Index

Salads

Sides

Soups

This 'n That

Vegetarian Main Dishes

Other Books from Images Unlimited Publishing

Yes, I want to order the following books. Please send me:

Quantity	Price per book	Total

Quantity   **Price per book**   **Total**

_____ *Cooking in the Midwest – A Collection of Favorite Recipes from the Heartland* $14.95   _____

_____ *From the Apple Orchard – Recipes for Apple Lovers* revised and expanded classic apple cookbook   14.95   _____

_____ *Apples, Apples Everywhere – Favorite Recipes From America's Orchards,* apple growers best recipes   14.95   _____

_____ *Healthy to the Core! Kids and Teens Low-Sugar – No-Sugar Apple Recipes,* kids love apples   14.95   _____

_____ *The Littlest Christmas Kitten,* children's full color storybook about the Holy Night and the cats' legacy   16.00   _____

_____ *Listening to the Mukies and Their Character Building Adventures,* gets kids thinking   12.95   _____

_____ *Cooking Around the Calendar With Kids — Holiday and Seasonal Food and Fun,* newly revised and updated   16.00   _____

_____ *Cooking Around the Country With Kids —USA Regional Recipes and Fun Activities,* take a tour through the USA   19.95   _____

_____ *Listening to Rural Midwestern Idioms/Folk Sayings* Entertaining guide to sayings and expressions   9.95   _____

_____ *Learning to Listen with Significant Others,* helps develop language and communication skills   14.95   _____

Subtotal   _____

Shipping:
Up to $50......$6.50
$51 –$100..... 8.95
+ $2 per book thereafter

Shipping   _____

Missouri residents add 7.975% tax   _____

TOTAL   _____

Name_____

Street_____ City_____ State_____Zip_____

Charge to ☐ Visa ☐ M/C Acct. #_____

Exp. Date: _____ Name on card _____

Or make check or money order payable to: Images Unlimited, P.O. Box 305, Maryville, MO 64468
800-366-1695

Visit us at http://www.ImagesUnlimitedPublishing.com and
http://www.CookingandKids.com/blog

Made in the USA
Monee, IL
03 November 2023